THE ULTIMATE MAC HANDBOOK
Connect with Your Inner Mac Genius

Jeff Graber

The Mac Support Store
www.macsupportstore.com

Published by The Mac Support Store Inc. 168 7th St, Brooklyn, NY 11215

First Printing 2009

ISBN 1-44869-303-9

Cover art: Dan Yeager
Editing: Susan Reed and Jeff Graber

TABLE OF CONTENTS:

TOP & SCREENSAVER, DOCK, EXPOSE & SPACES, INTERNA-
TIONAL, SECURITY, SPOTLIGHT, BLUETOOTH, CD & DVD, DIS-
PLAY, ENERGY SAVER, KEYBOARD & MOUSE, PRINTER & FAX,
SOUND, .MAC, NETWORK, QUICKTIME, SHARING, ACCOUNTS,
DATE & TIME, PARENTAL CONTROLS, SOFTWARE UPDATES,
SPEECH, TIME MACHINE, UNIVERSAL ACCESS

Ch. 1: Chapter One: From Skin to Core

The Essential Apple

Apple software updates

The first thing you should know about owning that milky new Apple—or the argent ones—is how to obtain software updates on your computer. You see, the sorcerers at Apple do their best to make sure your software fluidly runs within the magical wonders of your computer. Apple software updates are like little immunities to keep your computer not only virus free but also in fine fettle. That is, these updates fight off the things that could harm your Mac's health.

One of Apple's goals in software design is to make it not only trouble free, but moreover worry free. If you have an Internet connection that is both fast and functioning, then every-so-often you'll get a little box with a starry blue sphere encircled in an arrow that automatically opens upon starting your computer. All you have to do is push "OK" to install the list of items—from iTunes, iCal to iMovie and iChat—and then press OK to restart. After your Mac reboots, you're free to go on as expected.

Where do I find updates manually?

If after you read the abovementioned paragraphs you're thinking, *I don't ever see the automatic box asking me to update software. How do I find it myself?* Then do not fret. If, indeed, you never see such any sort of automatic update box appear randomly, then you can check for software updates yourself.

The most efficient way to do this is to simply click the little blue (or reflective silver) apple at the top of the computer screen. Scroll down and release select on *Software Update…*A few seconds later, you'll be able to accept or decline (check or uncheck) the updates that are listed below. After you accept, the computer does its probing—perhaps you'll have to peck your admin password too—and after downloading the updates, restart your computer. Viola!

If Software Update perturbs you because you have more computers than patience, then you can install the standalone installer, allowing you to update a number of computers downloading the update—whichever—one time. Tick here to install the Combo Update.

How do I know which version of the software I'm using?

This should be the same no matter your OS. Go to the little blue (or silver) apple again. This time, scroll down and release click About This Mac (probably the first item). Under the shiny, once-bitten apple, you'll see your system version. You can also see your processor speed and memory. There's even the option to check for system updates from here too.

How do I find Apple software or shareware that might be handy?

If you simply go to Google and type "shareware for Mac," for example, you'll surely find more than your Mac's memory can hold. Tick here to find the neatest stuff—tried, tested and thought through—for Mac. You can see the top downloads, see the editor's top choices and see the latest updates available. That said, there are lots of sites available, but this one is a one-stop shop.

If you want to go to the horse's mouth, platitudely speaking, then try http://www.apple.com/support/leopard to get support for all sorts of Mac's applications. Some software updates are available too.

Ch. 2 Chapter Two: From Spillage to Support

The Spotless Apple

Solving Mac Messes

A Mac mess is not something by and large caused my Apple or Mac. The problem is (most likely) yes, you, the user. If you are a Mac user, then you know the stability of 99% of Apple's programs, drives, applications and hardware. It's one of the reasons we all choose to use a Mac.

This chapter, then, is to inform you how to prevent losing information when something you've done—or not done properly—occurs. The main problem Mac users come across is not properly backing-up (if at all) those important files.

Here's some general yet helpful hints you might consider next time you multi-task and lose those critical dossiers.

What's the number one way to avoid a Mac (or self) meltdown?

Before you throw yourself or your Mac to the fire, you should take two precautionary steps: A.) Keep liquids away from the keyboard of either a desk- or lap-top computer. B.) Be sure to backup all your important files in at least two exterior locations. Let's start with "A.)." For "B.)," see the questions and discussion below.

The distinct reason people not only lose their data but also their computer is because of spillage. Spillage can be any liquid not intentionally spilled onto your computer. Spillage can range from morning coffee, lunchtime tea, and after-dinner spirits to baby's solid burp turned spit-up bile. The possibilities and despondent stories of a Mac's demise are always endless and never mild.

AppleCare won't really AptlyCare all that much if you destroy your computer with spillage. If spillage befalls your Mac, here's what you can do:

Be quick! Unplug your computer immediately. Shut it down and remove the battery from the back. Turn it upside down for at least 24 hours. This may keep the liquid from reaching the internal parts.

Some people suggest using a hairdryer while others say this is a bad idea. In either case, keep the computer off for at least a day to avoid the backup battery from corroding and ruining your Mac's internal hardware. It may be smart to take it to a Mac support store for diagnosis after such an incident.

How do I avoid future problems?

Now, we're getting to "B.)" and backing up. The best way to avoid future problems is to follow the ACT plan. The document can be an Excel or Numbers spreadsheet, a Word or Pages letter, or even a Power Point or Key Note presentation.

A – Keep your file(s) in Another location. In fact, keep them saved in at least two other locations, both on your computer and a removable disk. If you have an online Apple account, you can upload and save files here. Emailing files to your self is a nice way to access the document(s) anywhere, anytime. This can become tedious, however, after some time.

C – If you're in the middle of writing a document, be sure to Constantly back it up: in the beginning, middle and end. You never know when baby Jessie will upchuck her lunch of mashed sweet potatoes. Back up copies of your back ups as well.

T – Make several copies of the Type of document you want to save. Save the files as architect-plans-1.doc and architect-plans-2.doc and save them on your desktop and your documents folder, for example. Use an external hard drive whenever possible.

How do I best backup my important documents?

A CD or removable flash drive is at least an attempt at storing your files elsewhere. Making copies is a fine idea, but make sure to also keep the previous files even though you're backing up the newer ones. That is, be sure to save the previous file just in case the newly updated one is corrupted. You'll conceivable want to go back to the first one before the corruption occurred.

Where should I store my already backed-up important files?

Apple makes some handy gadgets to back up your hard drive. Have a look at your local Apple store or the Apple website. One of the latest gadgets is a simply external hard drive that automatically backs up your files when you plug in the USB cable. Everything that has been added or deleted is automatically updated. That's easy.

Or, a normal external hard drive works almost as well, giving you control of what is added to it or deleted and therefore updated.

Time Machine is a great tool too. However, it's intended for finding files that you've changed but would like to see the erstwhile versions. It should not be considered a backup or an archive for important files.

How often should I "spring clean" my Mac's directories and drives?

You might "spring clean" your computer about once a month or every other month. Run Apple's Disk Utility to repair any directories that might have been damaged. Be sure, of course, to back up all your files: ACT!

Moreover, use antiviral software frequently and be sure to use the updated versions. This is a simple process, sure to clean up any viruses that might be burrowing around.

Great! Is there anything else I should know from the experts?

Save all your disks and serial numbers in a safe and unified location. Don't download shoddy files labeled "free" from the Internet that you normally should pay for.

Choose shareware that has demonstrated wide user use with written reviews. You can check forums for updates and comments.

Additionally, buy software and hardware directly from the official online stores or Apple stores and dealers. Shoddy programs can kill your Mac faster than any spillage that might seep from any one of little Jesse's orifices.

Ch. 3 Chapter 3: From Know to Home

The Whole Apple

Buying & Choosing a Mac

Buying a Mac is sort of like having a newborn of your own: It's going to be an upfront expense; the more you love it, the more it will do for you; and, just when you thought you've seen it all, it gets better and better.

OK, it's not exactly like having your own child, but at least with a Mac you can choose its, well, character. Mac makes its simple, giving you a say in what you want and need versus nature surprising you.

With so many Macs out there, how do you know which *little one* to opt for? Well, this section will make it manageable, minus the difficulty of delivery. (Apple even does that, too!)

iMacs Peeled

Apple calls the iMac the "one-stop desktop." And, really, they aren't lying. If you're into a computer that has all-in-one capabilities, the iMac might be for you. It's best to think of this machine as both male and female as it has the right mix of hormones and parts to be both sporty and fetching at the same time.

The brain of this super child comes equipped with one of Apple's smartest moves yet—the Intel Core 2 Duo processors. Topping out at speeds of over 3 GHz, with 6MB of shared L2 cache, you'll be playing back vacation videos, burning DVDs, fighting of evil empires in realistic graphics, all the while touching up family photos in high-resolution. There are plenty of upgrades available too.

The iMac comes with a "SuperDrive." This CD or DVD drive enables you to burn movies onto a DVD or create double-layer DVDs for backup of files. You can even watch the movies on your TV.

Additionally, you can film those home flicks and snippets right from your computer. That is, the ultra-mini iSight camera has some intense picture quality, capturing the colors of the moment like never before. With iMovie, Photo Booth and iChat, you can stay in regular touch with your closest of friends.

Depending on which size of iMac you decide on, you'll get some nice standard drives and memories, with upgrades possible. The 20-inch iMac, for example, comes with 2.66 GHz of speed, 320 GB of drive space and 2GB of standard memory. Be careful, as this newborn may grow more muscly than you might be ready for.

Notebooks Peeled

As a soon-to-be proud parent to your new Mac, you may realize that you need more from a child. Expectations in the world today are higher for a young 'un than ever before. Decide now what you'll later demand. Would you rather have a *Jack-of-all-trades*? Or, the world's most *attractive prodigy*? Or a whiz, full of *sharp-witted intellect?*

Insofar as choosing an Apple notebook, you can have a choice in all three dispositions. The Jack of all trades **MacBook**, for instance, does it all with the new Intel Core 2 Duo processor and new Wi-Fi AirPort Extreme. If you're a stay-at-home Mac addict or an essay pumping, café sitting student, the MacBook can now be equipped with more than 250 GB of hard drive space and storage. But, at 1.08 inches and just under 5 pounds you can tote it anywhere.

If the MacBook doesn't trip you out, then the newest addition to the notebook family might. The *attractive prodigy* or **MacBook Air** is dubbed by Apple as the "World's thinnest notebook." At 0.16 to 0.76 of an inch and 3 pounds, and with no sacrifice to screen, keyboard or touchpad size, who can argue?

Also suited with the Intel Core 2 Duo and 80 GB 4200-Rpm hard drive, this prodigy is not only attractive but expeditious. However, if you're needing a DVD or CD drive and don't use wireless capabilities all that much, then the MacBook Air may not be for you. It is definitely built with the wireless world in mind. It's a fully realized, next-generation notebook.

Last but assuredly not least is the *sharp-witted* **MacBook Pro**. This intellectual notebook is not only highest-speed, but also incased in anodized aluminum. If the quondam notebooks seemed more like scratch pads, the MacBook Pro is the intense workbook.

You can either buy a 15- or 17-inch display screen and up to 2.6GHz Intel Core 2 Duo processor. Moreover, you have the pick of the litter with 200 or more GB and 5400-rpm hard drive. The MacBook Pro is built for professionals who want smokin' speeds combined with durability and practicality (a take to work then home Mac) all in one. At a possible 6.8 lbs, the MacBook Pro is built with smarts and power at the forefront of expectation.

Mac Pro Peeled

The Mac Pro is the grown-up version of computer power. These come with what Apple calls a Quad-Core Intel Xeon "Harpertown" processor. Accordingly, Apple claims that the new design—now standard—maintains the same energy efficiency as it predecessors.

Apple's promises don't stop with efficiency either. No, Apple stated recently that the new processors deliver improved bandwidth (25.6GB per second), nearly 20 percent greater than the former Mac Pros. If you require a lot of data crunching at once with image filtering or video effects, then you'll want nothing less than the Pro from Apple.

So, what does the Mac Pro mean to you? This computer is not for the nonchalant, at-home user. Unless your home-office requires the fastest and strongest computers, performing calculations and enhancements quickly, then you won't need Apple's Mac Pro. If you simply need something to check E-mails, listen to music, facelift photos and such, then you might look to the more appropriate notebooks, iMacs or Mac Mini.

One of the good things about the Mac Pro is update-ability. That means that your Mac can be upgraded to your specifications easier. Remember when cars used to be easy to work on? That is exactly what Apple has done with its new Mac Pro—with more horsepower updates than ever before. You can ad expansion cards, increase storage and memory with easy slide-in DIMM slots, all with little to no tools. The Pro comes with all kinds of USB and FireWire ports for your external toys.

Other Macs Peeled

By now you might be wondering what else Apple could possible proffer its customers? Amid rumors of discontinuing a crabappley-small version of the Mac computer, you might have to get your hands on the Mac Mini sooner rather than later. Though such minuteness makes you think *premature*, the Mac Mini is a Mini-fied version of an Apple desktop.

At 2 inches vertical, 6.5 inches wide and equally deep (and less than 3 pounds), the Mac Mini offers some nano power for home and office users alike. If in your formal life you were a pack rat and ran out of space, you won't have to fret just because the "Mini-ture" label. Yes, you'll be able to pack up to 160GB in a Serial ATA hard disk drive.

Moreover, the Mac Mini comes with a slot-loading SuperDrive (found in the MacPros and other power players) with double-layer support—both CDs and DVDs, writing at unheard-of speeds.

The processor and memory are just as advanced. Just because it's small doesn't mean it came with little parts. If the 2.0GHz Intel Core 2 Duo processor doesn't make you a believer in the power of small, then the 4MB shared L2 cache and 1GB of 667 MHz DDR2 SDRAM memory will zip and zap through multiple running programs simultaneously.

And, as surprising as too much packed in so small of a box seems, Apple gives you an 8 watt Fire Wire 400 port and four 2.0 USB ports. We all hate running out of these. Plus, you'll be running a standard Extreme Wireless networking to get on the Internet while listening to music through the built-in speakers.

Refurbished Macs Peeled

Who would dare eat an already-bitten Apple? If you recall, the Apple emblem is halfbitten, you see. A once-bitten Apple still makes for a well-running Mac. With the right pricing, you can save big bucks when you order your pre-owned Mac machine.

With 14%, 27%, and even 41% price cuts, Apple wants to clean out the closet of used equipment. Plus, you not only save money off the price, but you get an Apple certified product. This translates to a one-year warranty with the extension of three more years if you buy an AppleCare Protection Plan. Shhh!, Keep it a secret: This means that Apple stands behind even their refurbished equipment. You get the same coverage for your new-to-you computer as if you bought it at the never-used price.

Your Mac, Peeled Green

A few years back, Apple was under certain pressures by environmental groups and even popular websites about their lack of integrity towards a sustainable recycling plan. Today, those sentiments are a thing of the past as Apple moves forward with eco-friendlier methods of ridding you the customer and they the seller of eco-unsafe products. Here's just a couple of things they're doing.

Apple offers its *Free Recycling Program*. This program is only good, however, for cell phones and iPods. The good news here is that Apple will take back any model or manufacturer's products—even the older ones full of mercury, arsenic, PVC and lead (found in the cathode-ray tubes). All you have to do to recycle that cell phone or iPod is go to the Apple site, print off the mailing UPC and send it off. Apple will take care of the rest.

Apple furthers its eco-commitment by offering a exchange program. This method, though, requires you to first by any qualifying Apple computer—from an official retail store or online. After the purchase, Apple makes it easy.

If you buy your computer online, then you can opt to participate in *Apple's Recycling Program.* You can do the same from the store with any Mac specialist at the point of sale. Next, Apple will send you an E-mail with instructions and how to send in your computer. (Monitors and CPUs will need to be packaged separately, less than 70 lbs.) Then, take the packaged box to any FedEx location with a copy of the E-mail. Apple will do the rest, insuring that they do not send e-waste abroad. Steve Jobs even says Apple is always looking for ways to use high quality materials that are in high demand from recyclers— making it easier and better for everyone, globally.

Ch. 4 Chapter 4: From Little One To Leopard

The Upgraded Apple

Installing Leopard 101

Apple's new MAC OS X Leopard 10.5 (+ .2, .3 and climbing) is chock-full of hundreds of new bonus features. However, this doesn't mean that you'll have a hard time installing or upgrading it. Apple endeavors to make such installations simple, though some of the steps may at first seem more confusing than daunting.

Before a Leopard is ready to run (in the wild of the Intel processors), s/he must first be raised for action. Here are some helpful tips that might save you some time or headache with the first stages of Leopard-bearing. If this chapter doesn't help you, then click _this_— Apple's own Install Support Article for Leopard 10.5. (Though, this chapter is less confusing, mind you!)

Before we get to the install, check to make sure you can—and are ready—to actually upgrade.

◊ Check the system requirements for the newest version your installing or updating. You'll not only want minimum system requirements but also enough free space. If your Mac is too old, be careful not to ask for too much just because you install an updated OS. It may not run well.

◊ Check to see if all your software will run properly if you upgrade. Additionally, check manufacturers' websites, too, as updates are often available for free or for a small pittance.

◊ Clean up loose files and remove them from your desktop. Moreover, update your computer with all the software updates. Remember: Go the little blue or gray bitten apple in the upper left hand corner and select Software Update. Even if you did it yesterday, do it again as this puts the latest firmware onto your Mac.

◊ Back up your computer, as always.

◊ Never downgrade to an older MAC OS—Leopard to Tiger, for example. It won't work.

◊ Following the directions below, be sure to run the Software Update once

14

again to check for updates that came out after you purchased the CD/DVD.

Installing Leopard 102

We talked earlier about backing up your files and computer in previous chapters. Now, if you did not listen then, listen now: *Please take the time to back up your files and hard disk before installing any new programs or upgrades*—even if they're from Apple. A wrong push of a button or being stuck in a "loop" could cause datum (or all that data) to be cast away for good.

Installing MAC OS X Leopard is easy if you follow these 5 steps. Here's how:

1.) You can insert the install DVD while your computer is up and running and ON. This requires you to insert the DVD and then run the "Install Mac OSX.app." A big black X will appear in a gray box. Then, select the MAX OSX circular icon. You'll then click the "Restart" computer button (this may require a password). Your computer will reboot.

2.) Or, you can slip the DVD into the computer before you turn it on. Your Mac will know what to do from here automatically and you'll follow the steps provided.

3.) If and when your computer has (re) started—don't be surprised if this takes longer than usual—make sure to select the language you want. If you're reading this with ease, then you might want to choose *English*. You can even read more about Leopard as you go through these steps. However, it might be easier to read the rest of this article, as dilly-dallying leaves more chance for install errors.

4.) Next, you'll want to select the appropriate drive. Nine times out of ten, this will be the Mac HD*. You'll then hit Continue to press on. To begin, you'll have to press Install again. A usual (but bigger) gray box with a grayish X background appears. The blue "thinking" bar will show the installing process. Grab a bite or a drink as this does take some time, usually an hour or two, max.

5.) A welcome video will appear and then you can register. Henceforth, enjoy the new features.

You do have other installation choices, however. If you select *Options*, then there are three options (assuming you have OS X already on your system, there's really only two):

- Archive and Install: This puts a whole new copy of MAC OS X on your Mac HD. The existing files move to a "Previous System" folder. Most likely, too, you'll want to import your existing folders, settings, accounts and info to the newer running system. To do this, just tick the "Preserve Users and Network Settings" choice.

- Erase and Install: Back up your files. Then, if you so choose, you can erase your disk before installing the newer Leopard. Simply select this "Erase and Install" choice and then confirm by clicking "OK." There's even ways to partition and choose the format of the disk. However, this article will not delve into detail on this.

New With Leopard:

Apple lay's it on thicker with Leopard as they claim to have "300+ new features." Perhaps the mainstream Mac user won't need every new component on the new Leopard, but there are some attributes that make Leopard uncluttered and therefore user-friendlier.

This article can't possibly probe all 300+ features, but it will give you a slice of how Apple has made its Mac pie a bit sweeter. Here are a few of those slices and what they can do for the more typical user:

***Stacks* It Up:**

If you're the type who often misplaces your files, then Stacks will not only keep your desktop organized but also your mind at ease.

Stacks is a little nifty folder stored on the semi-transparent dock. All those file transfers, downloads from safari, icons, saved attachments and iChat downloads are saved in this folder.

In fact, Stacks organizes each file by time. That is, every time you download something new to your desktop, Stacks organizes the newest file closest to the dock and then expands the rest fan-like upwards with the oldest files last. You'll never have to sift through looking your most recent downloads. Plus, if there are too many files, Stacks will display your Applications in a grid instead of a fan. You can get to files and applications quicker than ever.

You can even create your own Stacks by a simple drag-and-drop of file(s) to the Dock. Then, by holding down the mouse key for a second, you can preset the new Stacks folder to sort by name, type, date added, modified, or created. You can also choose to have your files each time arrange in a grid or fan.

Finding in the Finder:

We all have an idea what finder is. It's Mac's way of allowing you to find your files in one place, more easily. With Leopard, however, Finder is just as much more versatile as it is pleasant.

With Mac's new finder, you get the same great choices of view-types— icon view, list view and column view—but with an added bonus— Cover Flow. Cover Flow allows you to flip through your documents and visually view them as-is. It's a lot like viewing your albums and covers in iTunes. Just the same, you can scan back and forth through your presentations, documents, files and pictures all in one painless mouse wave.

There are even little arrows at the bottom of each Cover Flow picture that allows you to flip through multiple pages within the Finder without opening and running the specific application that created it. If, for example, you want to flip through a picture album or review a movie, you can now do so right in the Finder application.

The sidebar of Finder, too, is organized just like iTunes. With Devices, Shared, Places, and Search For, you'll be able to quickly locate any file from the sidebar and open it within Finder. Together with Spotlight, you can access files not only from your personal computer but anything within your public home network over the Internet, even if you're far from home.

A Glance At Quick Look:

Quick Look allows you to view your documents (files, videos, movies, pictures and so on) without opening the Application that created it as well. If you're in the Finder window, for instance, and you want to open a thumbnail icon of a file without running an application, you can do so with ease.

Simply click the Quick Look icon or the space bar and your file zooms into frontal view. You can even resize the document or have it take up the whole screen if you'd like, and still the Application does not open. You'll be able to scroll through multi-page documents, and you can do it all from Cover Flow.

Travel Alongside Time Machine:

Time Machine is a revolutionary program that allows you to automatically back up and later find any file from your Mac computer. It, however, requires an external hard disk— the more space it has, the further back you can look in time. Time Machine can automatically save your files every minute of every day if you'd like.

Any time anything has changed on your Mac, Time Machine will back it up, on the hour for example. Time Machine makes recovery of files easy and chronological. You can then restore the erstwhile lost or deleted item manually or with Spotlight. Here's an example of how it works:

When searching for that long-gone file, you'll press the Time Machine button. Your desktop picture is now replaced with a starry image of file windows streaming back to infinity. There's a time line—which looks like UPC bar coding to the right—and arrows—pointing forward and backwards—permitting you to navigate through old to present folders. Then, you can use Quick Look to scroll through the old files to see if you've found what you were looking for. Once you've found it, you'll press Restore and Time Machine will restore the file to your present-day desktop. Neat, eh?

You Need Organize Spaces:

Most of us Mac users like to multi-task. We touch up and Email photos, play games, work on presentations and talk with iChat simultaneously. If you're like this ubiquitous Mac user, then Spaces will be your flotation device amid a sea of tasks.

It used to be true that if you pressed F9 or F10, you got mini-preview windows of all those activities you were working on. With Leopard, though, it's the same idea yet a better utilization. Now, you won't have all those activities jumbled together.

Turn on Spaces from the *System Preferences* by clicking on "Expose & Spaces." You'll be able to tick the enable square, thereby starting Spaces. From here, you can decide how many Spaces windows you want opened: 4, 6, or 8…it's your choice.

If you have six files opened from six different applications, for instance, you'll want 6 Spaces windows. You can easily flip through the Spaces windows by holding down the Control button and using the arrows (or hold down the Control button and select the appropriate Spaces number you want open). You can even drag and rearrange the activities to different spaces, whatever your preference. This allows for organization of all your activities under each specific Application.

More From Your Mail

The new Mac Mail answers our most important calls of nature. However, it used to be quite difficult to figure out just how to go about making your Mac Mail work. Do I have a POP, IMAP or Exchange server? What is the server address for incoming mail? These types of questions are not in the realm of user-friendliness. However, Leopard laps clean her cubs once again.

The first time you open your Mac Mail application, you'll be prompted as before. This time, though, you'll only have to answer some simple questions. Type in your name, Email address and password. You'll now skip the two to three other steps you used to have to complete and just click Create this time. Mail will now take over and carry out the rest.

Mail makes your daily life easier likewise. Now, you can take notes right within your Email account by clicking the yellow notepad at the top. After you've written your notes, you can drag and drop pictures and attachments right onto the screen notepad. The note will then appear as a new message in your inbox. You can then retrieve the note one week or one month (or longer) wherever you can connect to the internet. You can even select parts or pieces from the note, create or add it to an older to-do list and shoot it over to iCal.

If you like writing your E-mails with some pizzazz, then you can even create cool templates (like stationery) to send out as backgrounds whenever your E-mail is for a special celebration. There's more than thirty to choose from. And, within the stationery template you choose, you'll be able to drag and drop (and re-fit) the pictures from your iPhoto library.

Plus, the last deft addition to Mail is data detection. This allows you to simply run your mouse cursor over any data—such as names, telephone numbers, Email address and mailing address—and save it to an appropriate file, address book or other place. You can upload data or dates right into iCal.

iChat in Real Life

iChat, truthfully, has been about on par with the many other chat programs floating around out there. Within Leopard, though, Mac has made the iChat programs from business to pleasure and back again.

The new iChat is essentially the same platform, but this time you get to go to the theater. That is to say, the new iChat allows you to upload files, presentations, pictures and videos or movies as never before. Here this out.

If you choose to share a video or picture library, for example, the picture (or video) takes center screen, while the person your talking to becomes smaller. It has the same appearance as iTunes with Cover Flow operating. You'll be able to both share photos and see the same ones in real time, flipping back and forth in half- or full-screen mode (all the while you yak and blather!).

The new theater possibilities, there is more iChat can do, this time all for the sake of fun, withal. From distorting your own face like you're wandering through an old-fashioned hall of mirrors to adding crazy backdrops—simply by moving away for one second and coming back to the screen—you'll have hours of face-malleable mirth! If you want to add last year's Colorado hiking picture or the bluffs of the Buffalo River Trail to your backdrop, you can do so right from your own iPhoto library. Wherever you want to be (or don't), let the backdrops take you there.

If you'd like even more power and control, then iChat delivers this as well. By requesting and sending an invitation to a buddy or co-worker's computer, you can see, access and take over their computer from yours. This allows you to edit and work on presentations together in real time.

Surfing While On Safari

When we take that once-in-a-lifetime safari, we want to take our time and spot a few animals—panthers, tigers and leopards. When not on vacation, though, we want our Mac Safari to go as fast as possible, viewing as many web pages as possible in as little time as possible. The new Safari claims to be three to five times faster than other leading web browsers, namely Firefox and Opera.

The new Safari first allows user speed to reach new rates by switching, opening and dragging and dropping various opened web tabs. You can even integrate all those tabs or windows into one tabbed window, navigating through them not by guess but by sight.

Now, in Safari you'll get control over your PDFs. You can zoom, save or simply open it up in Preview. Plus, you can make text smaller or larger (in PDF or any webpage for that matter) by clasping the corner of the field and pulling or pushing. The page will reshape itself to fit the changes in text size.

If you'd like to add a webpage to your widgets on Dashboard, now you can. In one simple step—tick the Web Click button in the address section of Safari and select how you want the widget to show up— you'll be able to see our new widget next to your other Dashboard items. You can customize the look of the widget just like the others by flipping it over and adjusting the settings.

Back To Boot Camp, Soldier?

If you are the ambiguous, indecisive or divided type, then Boot Camp will surely sort you out. Boot Camp allows you to run Windows XP and Vista on your Mac. However, as Windows is wont to do, you will be susceptible to all those nasty viruses, bugs and worms. If your computer is affected, you may not even be able to access Leopard without a major computer overhaul.

That said, it's quite easy to set up Windows. The Boot Camp Assistant does it all for your. Your computer essentially becomes schizophrenic, with a fixed partition to keep all the datum separate. You can follow the wizard and the PDF manual as you install it. The Leopard DVD has all the requisite drivers you'll need to run Windows on your Mac. You can choose which OS to run after you push the power button by depressing the Option key and then settling on one.

Mastery in Parental Control

A new little filter—like the ones in your car—keeps bad things out of the viewing of your little ones. If the website it suitable for kids, then they load. If not, then they don't. If there's some mix up, you can even go into the system and change it.

Even if you're not around, you can now set up time limits on your family's Mac. By setting weekday and weekend hours of use, you'll be sure that your kids aren't wasting all their study time buying time with friends or social network pages.

You can even monitor what your kids search for, who they talk to, and which applications they've used. If you're connected to your home network—away from home too, for example—you can remotely access what they are doing and have done. A safer Internet keeps kids in a safer virtual environment (and lets you feel in parental control; and, control is fun).

Ch. 5 Chapter Five: From Progeny To Progressive

The Technologized Apple

Behind the New Features Curtain

As you just read, Mac offers so many more features with the coming-out of the new Leopard OS X. Though you were probably erstwhile convinced that Apple's Mac—no matter which you use—is superior, there is more to a Mac than features. Yes, that's right (in the best tout utterance possible), the wizard behind the curtain is in actuality nothing but better technology and design. Here are some of the mechanical workings that make Mac run so well.

Hereunder can give you a better understanding of the *whys* and *hows* of Mac's capabilities. Though you may not need the most power, you'll at least have a general idea of what is going on behind Mac and Leopard's newest features.

Understanding the various potential of the latest Macs will help you decide if its time for either a new Mac or an upgraded Mac. Plus, this can help you understand more of that computer lingo you may have been clueless about before. You'll be able to upgrade, download, maintain and troubleshoot by the time you finish this chapter.

Drill With 4 Times The Bit

That's right, with a Mac you can drill twice as much as before. Most personal computers over the last decade have been 32-bit. Apple, however, is the first company to put 64-bit computing into the new Macs, foreseeing and forging where computer technology is heading. You may ask, *What the heck is a bit?*

Most computers use binary numbers, combinations of 1s and 0s. This means that in one given cycle, the 32-bit processors doles out 232, or over 4 billion computations. Be that as it may, a 64-bit processor can compute 264, or over 18 quintillion calculations, well-nigh light speed comparatively speaking.

The 64-bit Mac, moreover, allows you to still run all the necessary

32-bit programs. New and old drivers will be compatible: Your printers, storage devices and PCI cards will, on the one hand, work seamlessly with the new technology, while, on the other, all those things will now run with increased throughput, essentially faster and better. You can use the newest Xeon processors, with speeds surfeit of 3.0GHz. Those internal mathematical drills taking place in your Mac's brain will work at breakneck speeds.

Do Tell, Why Intel?

A few years ago, rumors were afloat that Apple would start using Intel processors in their computers, forgoing IBM's PowerPC technology. In this case, rumors were reality, and Jobs (Apple CEO) made the announcement at the '05 developer conference and ended the speculation.

Apple still uses Intel Processors in all their computers today. Jobs said that Intel was on the road to designing better technology; that is, with an Intel Processor, you can get more done (in hours) per battery charge than other processors. After working out kinks in the heat created by the warp speeds, Mac lovers can now get up to eight cores of processing power in one CPU. Click _here_ to read all about it.

With the advent of these multicore processors, you've still got problems with performance. Just because, for example, you're more muscular doesn't necessarily mean you'll win the race; it takes efficiency and organization. With Leopard, though, such speeds are used more effectively, giving you more power plus user and application benefits.

HomeLand...er...HomeMac Security

Our lives these days are online. We buy our groceries, send flowers, pay the late credit card bill and Email friends and family. With such a networked life, security is of utmost importance. The last thing we need is a virus or bug attacking our hard drive; or worse, some thug stealing our identity and going on the fritz at the Rio Ritz.

Leopard makes it virtually impossible to steal your personal data from your computer or network. As long as you download the newest program and computer updates from Apple, you'll have the newfangled security available. Plus, Apple challenges hacktivist— some of the best in the business—to hack into their systems. Afterwards, Mac knows how to go about protecting its consumers.

Even when you download an application or file, Leopard can scan the item to see if it has been tampered with since it was last created. If so, you'll get the option to either run or stop the application from opening. That's like having armed security guards around your computer, awaiting your command.

Downloading To My Mac

Speaking of downloading, you may be at a loss as to how to A.) Download programs and files from the Internet to your Mac or B.) Check for downloads for your Mac from Apple. This will help keep that technology running with the degrees of satisfaction intended. Let's start with the latter, then the former.

If you don't trust your computer to know what's best for it, then you can simply jump on the Apple pages to see if there's any sort of software or firmware updates released. Maybe Safari has been unexpectedly quitting; or, iTunes seems to be shuffling your music into random assortments. To see if there are any updates for iTunes or Safari, simply click here to see all the latest upgrades in list format. You'll see another list of featured downloads to the right—most likely people are searching for the same upgrades, so you can easily find it on the sidebar—and an icon to run Software Updates automatically. You can also click here to see a list of top, recently added and featured downloads. There are widgets and movie trailers too.

If, however, you do trust your good ole Mac, then checking for software updates is simple (your computer should do this automatically once updates are available from time to time). In any case, you'll have to either select the blue or silvery half-bitten apple at the top left of your screen. From there, it's simple: highlight Software Update… You'll get a list of the newest software in a list. Follow the instructions (essentially pushing yes or no) and install any updates that may be available. You may have to type in your user password.

Forget Me Not: All About Passwords

Our online lives these days are all but brimming with passwords. The average computer user has three or more passwords to remember. Since we're supposed to change our passwords frequently, it's easy to forget, misplace or not know a password to something important.

Here's how to do almost everything you can do with passwords on Leopard. In order to start or log into your computer, you'll have to create a password—rightfully called your account password. If the computer is yours, or you are its administrator, you are in control of not

24

only your password, but also all the other users' passwords.

Changing A Password

This procedure is quite simple, and is nearly the same for Tiger as it is for Leopard. Your first move is to get into your *Accounts*. In order to do this, you must click on the Apple menu at the top. Then, choose *System Preferences* and then *Accounts*. Voila, you're there.

Next, you'll open the password pane, where your accounts are stored. If this is locked, all you have to do is push the little padlock icon and type in your administrator password. The padlock should unlock and give you complete, omnipotent access. You'll then do what you have come to do—click *Change Password*.

Now—I know this typing and retyping gets old, but you haven't seen the half of it— you'll have to enter your current password in the Old Password portion. You can either get some assistance in choosing a complex arrangement of letters and numbers to make your new password or you can do it yourself. You'll then see if it's a secure choice or not. After, type in your new password. You'll have to do it twice in the verify section again. I know, I know.

If you're the kind of person who runs around the office screaming, "Where's my glasses?" as they rest upon your head, then you better type in a password hint in the respective field. This hint will be given to you if you screw up your password more than three times. Click Change and your old password is now modified to the new one.

Changing An Administrator Password

If you are the administrator and would like to change your administrator password, then you can do that by following all the abovesaid steps plus one. Make sure to go to the Keychain Access* and change your login password there too (it must be the same as your administrator password). This will make your keychain unlock when you log in using your administrator name and password.

*In order to change your keychain password, open your Keychain Access in the Utilities folder, placed in the Application folder. Then, click Open Keychain Access. You'll have to go into Edit and Change Password for Keychain. You may have to type in your password again. Type the new password and then verify it by typing it again. Get help with it, choose it, remember it, write it down, sing it to your memory and then click OK. OK, you're done.

Changing A User's Password

Let's just say little Tameeka forgot her password again. Most likely, she is not the administrator, so you'll have to help her out, being her eldest sibling or parent and all. Once you're logged into your own (administrator) accounts, then the rest is very similar to above.

You'll do the same as above but this time you'll be given a list of the users allowed on the computer. Select the username. In this case, Tameeka's username is Tamee. Select it. If you've got an older OS version, you may have to tick the Reset Password button. If not, simply enter the new password and verify it. Click OK and Tameeka can get on with her favorite math games.

Can't Log In After You've Install An Upgrade?

Before you upgrade your Mac with the latest software—say Leopard 10.5—you should make sure all user accounts have a password for the log in*. If not, you may not be able to later log into the same account even though there is no password once Leopard is installed. There is a mending method, though, if you did not have a password on a user account beforehand.

You'll have to first put the Leopard Install DVD into the DVD driver. From here, select the Utilities menu. Then, to add a password or change it, choose Reset Password once you've selected the malefic user account. Try to always have passwords for every user account.

*If the user account had a password before, and you still are having trouble, it's because the password was probably more than eight characters (created on an earlier OS, for example). Just follow the same steps above to fix the problem.

Changing A Master Password (Are you the Master?)

If you have accounts protected by FileVault, then you can create a master password to allow intimate access of all user accounts. A master password is quite important. Once you lose or forget it, there is no way to get any information from your computer ever again. Scary, eh?

To create your master password, go back into *System Preferences* in the Apple menu. This time, however, you'll click *Security* (instead of Accounts). After clicking *Security*, choose *FileVault*. You may have to unlock the little padlock again with your admin password. Then, click *Set Master Password*. Type it once to set it and again to verify it. You can have the password assistance help you if needed. Type in a hint if you need one. Then click OK. Your master password is set and ready.

Troubleshooting: My Mac Won't React

You sit down with your morning brew to do some morning catch up on the Mac but you don't hear the all-familiar chime (Pavlov's dog would be upset). You press some buttons again and again but nothing happens—a black semi-reflective or frozen screen reflects your dropped jaw and the sun coming through the window—but nothing else. Your Mac just won't react. Here are some things to try.

So, you've made sure your computer is plugged in, that the power is on and functioning right? So, if you don't hear a darn thing—say no fan or drive sounds—and no lights whatsoever come on, you may have a chance to fix it manually.

iBook & PowerBook

Before we get into a PMU (Power Management Unit) reset, first try a few of these steps. If the computer is just sitting there (with the color wheel spinning, perhaps), then just try to manually force quit by depressing Option-&-Command-&-Escape simultaneously.

Ok, no whammy. Try a restart by depressing Control-&-Command-&-Power button. And if this still leaves you hanging and a bit worried, it might be time to force your computer's shut down by pressing the Power button for nearly 10 seconds. If still no reaction, then it's time to start your PMU. You'll have to click *here* and choose which iBook or PowerBook you have and follow the instructions carefully.

Mac Mini & iMac

To reset the PMU on the Mac Mini and iMac, the process is the same. The first necessary step is to unplug the cords from your computer. This means all of them: any speakers, any monitors, printers, mice and especially the power cord. After you've done this and checked it over, use a watch and let the computer rest for 10 seconds.

Now comes the tricky part. It may be helpful to have a helping hand for this task. What you'll want to do is have the computer ready to be plugged in, near the wall outlet. Next, have your finger or your helper's finger hovering over the power button. On the count of three (1-2-3), plug in the computer while pushing and holding down the power button. As your hand lets go of the power cord, let go of the power button.

If nothing happens, you've done something right. Now, press the power button as you normally would if your computer was simply shut down. The computer should turn on as normal. Now, you'll have to reset all the internal workings—clock, date, calendars—of your computer. If this doesn't work or your video no longer displays, then you'll have to take your Mac into a certified Mac shop for consultation.

Mac Pro

The Mac Pro is a little different than its other Mac cousins. Namely, you'll try something here that won't reset your PMU but your SMC (System Management Controller). Specifically, the SMC controls all the power doohickeys. It's nothing but a small chip but does so much to signal to your computer's components when to turn on, wake up, go to sleep and when to kick on the fans. Like the chips in choco-chip cookies or the chips served alongside your fish, this chip is just as compulsory: Mac & Chips, please.

The first thing you'll want to do is shut down your computer. Do it from the Apple menu or force quit if you have to (or hold down the power button till your screen turns black/off.)Next, make sure all those cables are free of the computer jacks. You'll also want to take out the power cord. Try and wait at least 15 or 20 seconds. Use a watch if you are impatient.

Now, make sure the power cord is connected to your computer. This time, you won't hold down the power button. You'll simply plug the computer in and leave the power button alone. You'll want to plug it in and then it's OK to plug in your keyboard and mouse and printer and such again. Then, turn on your computer by pressing the power button.

MacBook, MacBook Pro & MacBook Air

These three little laptops are a bit different than the aforesaid computer. Again, you'll reset the SMC—(again) the little chip that governs power to the backlighting, hard disk, going to sleep and waking up, trackpad and charging. Yes, the SMC is given a bit more power in the laptops.

At any rate, you'll want to shut off your **MacBook** or **MacBook Pro** computer. Take away the plug-in adapter and remove the battery from the bottom. Then, hold down the power button for at least five seconds and then release. Now, put the computer's battery and power adapter back into the computer. Now, press the power button as you normally would. The computer will turn back on, but the SMC will be rebooted.

The **MacBook Air** computer is a little easier and doesn't require all the stuff to be removed. First, simply make sure the computer is off. Now, all other Macs require that the computer be removed from the power source. However, with the MacBook Air, you'll want to plug it in to the power source.

You must press <u>Shift</u> + <u>Control</u> + <u>Option</u> and the <u>Power Button</u> at the same time. The trick here is to think with the left side of your brain. That is, you'll have to press the mentioned buttons but the ones on the LEFT side of your computer. After pressing these four buttons and waiting five or so seconds, push only the <u>Power Button</u> as you normally would. Your MacBook Air will start again.

Mac Maintenance: A Shiny Apple

- The first thing to do is to check for Apple software updates at least once or twice per month. This will keep you combating the super-viruses of the here and now. You can set this up automatically.
- Make sure all your file names have exact names. If you're one to use spotlight, for example, it's much easier to find "Business Program.doc" rather than xlfgt.doc, for example. Use files and folders and stay on top of them.
- If you have many files you want to keep but no longer need, then try to save them as archives. Delete any files you don't want or need.
- Back up your files again and again. If you have Time Machine, all the better.
- Make sure to clean the dust from the screen, keyboard and outside of the computer. Dust can stick to fans and cause overheating.
- Don't use chemical cleaners and do use a dry, soft dampened clock to wipe off your computer. If you keep your Mac clean, it will gleam with more speed and last a lot longer. And, for goodness sakes, clean off the fingerprints from the keyboard. It may be wise to dust off your Mac every week or two, depending on your dustiness.

Ch. 6 Chapter Six: From Uncertain to Undoubted

The Applications Apple

Certain Answers to Application

An ordinary Mac comes freshly wrapped in an Apple box. Probably shipped from California, you've opened the new MacBook Air or Pro and goggled at it long enough. You've probably even tinkered and futz with as many things as you know how. The new Leopard, however, may have left you dizzy with misapprehension. But don't worry. This chapter will go over some of the cool programs in your Applications folder.

There's neither enough time nor enough memory space to tell you about all of the Applications you could possibly buy or add to your new or updated-to-Leopard Mac. However, this chapter will go over some of the more ubiquitous programs that come preinstalled on every Mac.

Whether you have Leopard installed or not, this chapter can better help you understand some of the more common problems—nay, not problems but more like misunderstandings—that Mac users sometimes tax over. It's time to go from being Uncertain to Undoubted. Here's what's up with your Mac's Applications (in alphabetical order):

Applications & Answers

Address Book Allows you to know more about a person than you probably ever wanted to remember. Not only can you Email, visit a contact's website or chat directly from an Address Book card, you can jot down their chat names, names of important people in their life, phone numbers, and addresses: mom, dad, partner, dog, puppies and other persons. The list is endless, truly. Plus, you can print out a quick address label to send them their birthday present. Mac just brings everyone closer, maybe too close.

Hurdle 1: At any rate, the Address Book Application is a nifty tool, especially because you can synch it with all your other Mac OSX computers in your house (as long as you've got a .Mac account, that is). People often report having trouble figuring this out. It's quite easy. Here's how:

- Go into your Address Book and select Preferences
- Select the "Synchronize my contacts…" button

- If you haven't, sign into your .Mac account
- Now, in the .Mac preferences, you'll need to tick "Sync"
- Choose "Synchronize with .Mac
- You'll then choose how often you'd like this to be done (automatically)

Hurdle 2: Let's just say you thought you ticked the right box when you installed the Leopard upgrade to your Mac. Perchance, however, you accidentally chose "Erase and Install," or didn't choose to "Preserve Users and Network Settings." If this sounds at all likely, then you're contacts did not import to the Address Book. Here's how to do it (as long as you hitherto had version 10.2 or higher):

- You'll have to quit the Address Book application
- In your previous home folder, you'll have to search for the address book name under the library
- It will look something like this: ~/library/application support/ addressbook
- You'll simply copy that folder into the same plalce in your new home folder
- This should leave you with all your contacts in the new Address Book folder

Hurdle 3: Maybe you've experienced another hurdle with the Address Book. This one involves problems with importing a contact to your Address Book. If you've tried and tried to import a contact to no avail, then it's time to check what kind of "document" it is.

- You'll have to go to the Finder and choose the document.
- Then Open File and Highlight Get Info.
- You'll then see where the file came from: Firefox, Netscape, vCard, Palm Pilot, iPod, Outlook and so on.

If your file is a CSV file, then you should have no problem. If you do, however, just go through the same steps above with some supplementary steps: Go to File and Get Info again. This time, choose Read & Write from the "You Can" window. You should either be able to choose the contact to add here or change the file tag.

Boot Camp is the program you've probably heard about: Running Windows (XP &/or Vista on your Mac). Yes, it's true. It's now possible to run not only Windows on your Mac but those sometimes hard-to-find (made only for Windows) programs. You'll have to buy both Windows and the software in order to use it on your Mac. And, your Mac will now be susceptible to all those viruses and worms out there.

Hurdle 1: Want to set Windows or Mac OS X as my default running system, but can't. There's a couple ways to do it. First, you can set this up through the Boot Camp control panel or the Startup Disk preferences. Essentially, you'll have to set it up from either Mac or Windows.

- Assuming your in Mac OS X, you'll have to choose System Preferences under the half-eaten Apple menu
- Then, highlight Startup Disk
- Now, simply choose which OS you want
- It will stay this way by default once you turn on your computer
- You can choose which one when you start up your computer too (hold down the Option key when you push the power button and then choose one)
- Or, when you have one or the other running, you can select to change OS by restarting

Hurdle 2: Essentially, you've got to treat your computer as two different computers if you choose to put Windows on it. What you'll be doing, in effect, is partitioning your computer's brain in half. If you've done this, and now realize you either don't need Windows or you just want it off your computer, there is a way. Make sure you save anything you'll need from the Windows partition before doing this. Once it's done, all will be lost.

- First, make sure that no other applications are running
- Log anyone out of the computer
- Now, in the Application folder, choose Utilities and then choose Boot Camp Assistant
- You'll then have to select a rather daunting command: "Restore startup disk to single volume"
- You might have to choose which internal disk Windows was created on (only one of them will be partitioned with Windows)
- When you choose "Create or remove a Windows partition" the rest is easy
- Find the disk with Windows
- Then pick "restore to a single Mac OS partition"
- Voila

iCal is essentially an interactive daily, weekly, monthly and yearly calendar and to-do list, organizing your life, your mind, right down to your spirit. You can have one or many iCalendars on the same computer to see who is doing what when. It can keep the small business or family on the same page, week by week.

Hurdle 1: If you've just installed Leopard and opened the Calendar or Mail widgets, then you may have some empty calendars (perhaps the "Home" and/or "Work" calendars). This has been a bane case for iCal users 3.0 with Leopard 10.5. Here are some options, though they are not the best if you don't have backup.

- You can copy your iCal manually, one by one (ug!)
- You can do the same automatically, but it will take some manual work
  1. You can copy your calendar data with "Users/~/Library/ Application Support/iCal"
  2. If this works only part way, (Quit iCal) then copy "Users/~/ Library/Calendars" to your desktop and reopen iCal
- If you we're lucky enough and had the foresight to backup your iCal, then you can access your backup by going to File and highlighting Backup Database
- Your iCal information should be available next time you start iCal

Hurdle 2: Perchance your Home and Work Calendars show up but your To Do list or your Events do not. Try the following checklist to see if you can restore or find them (easy to hard):

- Check to see if the Event or To Do is ticked with checkmark
- Check Time Zones and Dates (iCal and Computer's)
- Search for the Event in the search field (at the bottom)
- If you have the Month viewing open (not day or week), and you only see some of the items, see if there are ellipses. If so, click those or change your viewing to see the entire list
- Your items may be scrolled. Scroll down or up until you see your items (check to see they are listed on the correct times)

iChat is a popular Internet chat tool. It used to be only so-so popular as there's so many other chatting platforms out there. However, the new-thus-improved iChat has more features than any other chatting program, bar none.

There are all sorts of video effects and backdrops for starters. You can make the background change: look like you're in front of a waterfall at Yosemite National Park or on the moon, for example. And, the fun doesn't stop there: You can discuss and present slideshows, watch movies simultaneously and share/swap business notes. You can even remotely access and control your partner's computer via a network or over the Internet. Whether using Leopard-to-Leopard or Leopard-to-Tiger or -Panther, you'll not lose iChat's newest components.

Hurdle 1: If you're not sure how to add one of your contacts from your address books to your buddy list (or to start from scratch adding your contact to the address book and then to the buddy list), here's how. The address book keeps all your friends, lovers, pets and people organized in your life. The buddy list, what's more, enables you to see when they're online (signed in).

- Touch your mouse pointer to the plus + symbol and click it once while your in the buddy list portion
- The cards of your address book should appear
- Choose the person from this book and they will be added as a buddy
- If they don't already exist there, then click the "New Person" button
- Type in as many aliases or screen names your contact uses
- Whenever they sign in, you'll be able to see them
- If a new person is added to your buddy list, an Address Book card will automatically be made for them
- You can access your buddy list from anywhere in the world

Hurdle 2: Maybe you have either not known or figured out that you can manipulate your video picture with video effects. You can appear in black and white, as a picture negative, as a pop art album cover or as a cartoon and more.

Some people have suggested that figuring out how to use the Video Effects option is a bit tricky but really it's not. Here's how:

- You should be chatting with one, two or more buddies to use video effects in iChat
- Go up to the menu and choose the Video option
- There will be a phrase called Show Video Effects; choose it
- There will be a miniature version of all the choices you'll have (like on Photo Booth)
- The effect you choose will change the way you appear to your friends, but not the other way around

- If you want to preview a video effect, when you do so, your buddy will see it
- To go back to the real you, just click on the original Video Effect

Mail makes mailing an Email into mailing Entertaining-Mail. Namely, Mac's Mail makes Emailing ordinary Emails not only fun and entertaining but also memorable.

With Leopard, you'll have a triad of ten personal stationery choices. Also, you can write yourself notes (instead of Emailing yourself), adapt To-Do lists all the while keeping track of important Emails and adding dates to your iCalendar. Being organized used to be boring. Mac's Mail makes it a ball.

Hurdle 1: We discussed the stationery feature of Mail above. Now, though, you should learn how to access them.

- You'll have to choose *File* and then *Get Info* after you've chosen a file
- You'll then select the *Stationery Pad* box
- You can use the same templates over and over again
- You will always have the template, even if you change the file

Hurdle 2: Sometimes you'll log onto Mail and you might have an Error message or other message prompt you. With all the acronyms out there, it's best to have an idea what they all mean. Here are the types of servers and types of mail divulged:

- SMTP server is a *Simple Mail Transport Protocol*. This initially receives your messages and sends them across the WWW. These are good for security as they generally only accept messages from an address on the same network. If you have trouble with the SMTP or get a message containing this acronym ("cannot send...SMTP...") when you try to send Email (or the Send button is not pressable) then you'll need to call your provider.
- POP (*Post Office Protocol*) is Email stored until you retrieve them online, often downloading them to your computer. Sometimes, you can access this only from your computer and not anywhere else.
- IMAP (*Message Access Protocol*) mail, on the other hand, is mail that is stored on your ISP's server. You can access your

Email messages anywhere, anytime, the world over. This type of mail is more flexible and convenient should you use many computers in many locations. Sometimes you can contact your server provider and ask to use either POP or IMAP.

QuickTime comes pre-installed on your Mac under the *Application*'s folder. You can upgrade for a few dollars, however, too. The new Quicktime for Leopard uses H.264 video quality standards. As of now, this is as good as mobile devices (MPEG 4 HD-DVD and Blu-Ray) get. With Quicktime, you can share the files easier over Email, put movies on most of your iToys and create the highest quality movie H.264 content.

Hurdle 1: You want to play part of a movie or just select (part of) it, here's how:

- Most likely the selection markers are hidden when you aren't using them
- To choose a section of the movie, you can move these markers in and out
- When you do so, the area you select will turn a shade darker
- You can edit the selection by choosing a marker; use the arrow keys to move it
- If you want to watch the selection, go up to View. Highlight the Play Selection Only.
- Press Play.
- When you're ready to move on to watching the rest of the movie, go back up and de-check Play Selection.

Hurdle 2: You'll need to know your choices if you want to put your movie on the Internet for the world to see. Hopefully the people involved in the movie don't mind either. Here are your two choices and the differences in each:

- HTTP is a way to deliver your movie so that other people have to download the movie (and thus save it) to their computer. They'll have to download it and then watch it.
- If you don't want others to have saved copies of the movie on their hard disk, then you can use the Real Time Stream option. This is done from the Quick Time Server. This is nice because others can watch the video in real time if need be. If you have a live performance to debut, for example, you can use Real Time

Stream to show the video. This won't take up any hard disk space on others' computers either.

Safari, as you probably know, comes on your Mac and is Apple's web browser baby. Apple says its 3xs faster than other competing browsers, though many factors such as computer speed, connection speed and system configurations make a big difference.

Hurdle 1: You may try to open up a URL or webpage and the page says something like "Temporarily Unavailable." Whether you're using Safari or not, try these simple steps to get you back surfing the World Wide Web Wave again.

*   Wait some time before going back to the page and test it again
*   Try resetting your web browser
*   Try emptying the cache and cookies
*   Make sure you're online. Sometimes if you're using Bluetooth or Airport you might lose a signal for a while
*   Try typing in "/index.html" at the end of the URL Address
*   Try retyping the web address. These days, one word web addresses are harder to come by. So, if the phrase or sentence is misspelled, you want to try and spell it right. (Http://www.l8rallygator.com versus Http://www.l8terallygator.com for example)
*   If all else fails, try to Email the site administrator and detail your suffering

Hurdle 2: One of the ways to make web surfing less stressful is to get rid of all those popup windows. Safari gives you two ways to do this. And, unlike some other unsophisticated web browsers, you'll be able to click and open links without disarming your pop-up blocker.

*   Go into *Preferences...* under the Safari option at the top. Depending on your Safari version, you'll have to dig around until you find the *Block Pop-up Window* option. A checkmark should appear next to it once you've selected it and essentially turned it on.
*   Or, go into *Preferences...* again and find the *Security* option. Afterwards, click the select the *Block Pop-Up Windows* option.
*   Be very careful as some web pages login screen appears as a Pop-Up Window. You'll have to disable the blocker if this is the case in order to log in.

Time Machine automatically backs up your files, photos or anything else you do with your Mac. You can essentially go back in time to recover any version or copy of any file you've done. Say you want a picture before you edited it, accidentally turning it yellow. You can go back and retrieve the pre-yellow photo by using Time Machine. Plus, you can use Time Machine to save your work automatically whenever you want to. You'll need an external back up in order to do this, however.

Hurdle 1: In order to start using Time Machine, you'll have to go through some simple steps.

- Go to the beloved Apple menu above. If you click on System Preferences you'll see an option for Time Machine. You'll want to slide the switch to the ON position
- Once you have an external disk—ipod or iDisks even—you'll have to Change Disk and choose one. This is where you'll be storing your "old" versions of things. Click Use for Backup, Voila!

Hurdle 2: What happens if I run out of space on my Time Machine backup? Well, there are a few things you can do manually, but Time Machine usually takes care of this by starting to delete the oldest versions of files to make room for the newest. If not, try these options:

- Apple suggests buying and using a new backup disk once the first is full. If you want to keep using the current one, however, you can. You can manually go through and erase files or have Time Machine do it automatically
- The best way to backup your files is to not backup as many. That is, you probably don't need to backup every little thing, every little minute. This will fill up your backup disk quickly. One of the best things to do is to back up movies, photos and larger files on the Internet—say a photo directory, for example. If you're only backing up and saving Keynotes or Pages documents, it will take Time Machine a long time to fill up (depending on your gig). Set the automatic save for every day or hour to save even more room for the future.

Ch. 7 Chapter Seven: From Dock To Dash

The DED Apple

Understanding DED: Dock, Exposé and Dashboard

The Mac Dock is a display of icons you can position anywhere on your Mac screen—bottom, right or left. You can affix or remove any of your preferred Mac Application icons to it. Programs such as Safari, iTunes, iCalendar, Pages and the Trash are just a few examples. The Mac Dock was first introduced with the arrival of Mac OS X. The icons ripple as the mouse is run over, magnifying the icons. Moreover, you can set the Dock to either always be visible or always hide. The animation of the Dock is the basic idea that the Mac can be visibly appealing, useful and unique all at once.

If you have any folders, files or Applications you'd like to add to the Dock, you can do that at any time too. With Leopard, the Dock has advanced to new stages of both importance and user-friendliness. The Dock, additionally, is Apple's way of saying, "See how easy this is." You have ease of access and quicker startup with the Mac Dock system than ever before.

The Dock

Mac's Ship docks On The Dock

Mac's Dock is where all the Application ships are moored. In other words, if you need any of your Applications lickety-split, then the best place to put them and have them ready is the Dock—a ship ready for rescue!

Mac's Applications dock on the Dock, so to speak, because this is what aesthetically sets the Mac apart from the PC—that it is visually appealing and clutter free, with ease-of-use and mindfulness ahead of simply listing lists of applications. At any rate, the Dock is the place where you should, really, dock all those Applications you use most regularly, steadily adding and subtracting icons when you need them and don't. We'll talk about that here in a jiffy.

For now, here are some basic how-Tos to get you started with your Dock. If you've used it for a while, then read on: Perhaps there's a chance you'll not only learn something useful, but also something cool. (It's always so much fun to show your PC-user friends the refreshing things of your Mac.)

Keeping Your Dock Afloat

There are a lot of ways to arrange your Dock with the new Leopard OS X. In fact, you should do so in order to keep it all not only visually appealing but also keep Applications easy to find. Insofar as the Dock goes, you'll probably have all sorts of Applications docked there for accessibility purposes. So, arrange your icons thematically or in some way that you know where things are kept.

In order to get one of the Applications to open from the Dock, you'll have to tap the icon with your mouse one time. The icon will then bounce as if excited as the Application opens.

If you'd like to open iCalendar, for example, then run your mouse over the icon of the mini-calendar. Once you wave the mouse over it, it should magnify (if not, we'll tell you how in a moment). In any case, select the small calendar and it should begin bouncing. The calendar opens and it and any other Applications you currently have running will have a blue light beneath it. If you'd like to change the Application but still keep it open, then just tap the icon in the Dock. This Application, then, will be the one on the front of your screen, ready for you. You'll be able to see which Application is running by looking at the Application name next to the silver Apple up in the menu bar.

So, now you may be wondering why certain Applications appear in the Dock when you didn't put them there. You can hide these at anytime by right clicking (ctrl + keypad key = mouse right click) the icon and choosing "Hide." You can generally only hide the icons that appear while running, not the main icons you always have listed in the Dock. The more Applications you have running (say you have eight Pages documents opened and minimized) the longer your Dock will be. This might be a time to hide them if you're not using them for a while.

Drag & Drop Off At the Dock

I know this is something you'd probably like to do to your kids when they misbehave, but dragging and dropping off at the dock is simpler than that, and won't get you into any trouble. If you keep your Mac's Dock at the bottom of the screen, then those Applications you open and minimize will appear left of the trashcan. You'll always find folders and other minimized icons to the right with Applications to the left.

If you'd like to change where these Application icons appear, you can simply drag them by hovering the mouse over the icon, holding down the right key or mouse keypad and lifting and dropping it somewhere else along the dock. The newest version of Leopard places a crosswalk-type translucent emblem dividing the icons. If you want the icon to disappear from the Dock, all you have to do is drag and drop it again, but this time place the icon on the desktop. It will puff into smoke and be gone. It is, however, still in your Applications folder for later. Once you're done using an Application that is not normally housed in the Dock, it will also disappear. How convenient, eh?

Magnification *ON* At the Dock

Told you we'd get to this. It's very easy to turn ON and OFF the magnification of the Dock. Likewise, you can easily change the degree at which your Application icons magnify. Go up to the Apple menu at the top. Scroll down to *Dock* and *Dock Preferences...* Here, you'll see all the options: size, magnification and position. Change them (and test them) and then you're done.

Dock Trash: Throwing Away, Empting and Shredding

The next time your honey yells, "Take out the trash," you'll be able to do so with the push of a button. When you retort, "Done!" she'll give you a reward for such good behavior. Little does she know, however, that the ease with which you emptied the trash occurred on your MacBook. That's right, with the push of a mouse button, you can throw files away, empty the trash or shred it for good.

Just like any rubbish bin, the Mac trash bin let's you know when it's full and when it's empty. By looking at the Trash icon in the Dock, you can see when there's rubbish piled high. On the contrary, if all you see are the crisscross wires of the bin, then the Trash is already empty.

The Trash is really not a trash insomuch as a folder to hold files or folders or documents you think you may not need. If you drag a file, for example, from the desktop to the Trash bin, then it will go inside, making a "throwing away" noise as you do. If you end up needing this same file later, all you have to do is click on the Trash bin and you'll be able to see its contents. Drag the file from the trash to the desktop to restore it.

You can empty the trash after it has built up waste files by right clicking with your mouse and selecting *Empty Trash*. Or you can click on *Finder* and *Empty Trash* from there. Either one is just as efficient. (Remember: If you don't have a mouse, a right click can be substituted by holding down the ctrl + keypad key = mouse right click.)

If you've got some files you just have to make sure no one recovers or ever sees, then you can *Empty Trash* more securely. To do so, go to the *Finder* at the top of your screen. After selecting it, scroll down till you see *Secure Empty Trash* and select it. This act is essentially like shredding documents. Unless someone has a lot of extra time and some scotch tape, then it's not likely they'll ever recover the data. It's actually eliminated and written over and over again until the info is unintelligible. Finally there's a safe way to get rid of your past pole dancer pictures.

Exposé Exposéd

Exposé came out less than eight years ago with the advent of Mac OS X. Exposé allows you to search through opened applications on your desktop without mousing around for them. If, for example, you have nine Applications running, at the push of a button, Exposé arranges those in a mini-fied version on your screen. By scrolling over them, a grayed-in text appears detailing what it is you're pointing to. Exposés main use is to help you find opened Applications quickly, switching back and forth with ease.

If you have several windows open under one Application, and would like to see only those, then you can use the defaulted F10 key. This Application will be at the front of your screen while other Applications and files will be shaded in the background.

By pressing F9, you'll get a similar effect, but see all the Application windows at once. All of these, too, will be shaded except the one your mouse is over. Click on the window to bring it to the forefront. If you need to get to your desktop amid all the clutter, press F11. This clears all Applications and windows from your screen so you can access your desktop. Juxtaposed with Spaces, Exposé becomes more organized, giving you the power to arrange Applications and windows to your preferred visual settings.

You can change these F-Keys around if you'd like by clicking on the Apple in the menu. Select System Preferences and then select the Exposé picture. You'll be able to rearrange the way your files appear and the command keys you'd like to change to.

The Dashboard

Pellucid Widgets At Your Fingertips

What's a widget, you may have asked yourself. Used as a synonym with gadget, the word Widget came about in the latter part of the 1930s to describe something either unspecific or unsure, usually with technology or machinery.

The Mac Widget, however, is a bit more specific in a general kind of use. To say it another way, Widgets are Mini-Me, scaled-down versions of bigger Applications—OR— are (little "a") applications used on the periphery of other projects (perhaps not good enough to warrant their own [big "A"] Application icon). Using Pages as your main Application while using the Translator Widget to help define some of your words is one case in point. In any event, the Widget is a dummy-downed version of a big "A" Application and a less important application. The Widgets are used when you open up Dashboard on your Mac.

Some Widgets, as abovementioned, are Mini-Me versions of larger Applications. This means that if you want to listen to iTunes without opening the full Application, you can simply open the widget to change your music. If you need a quick Google search but don't want to open Safari, then you can do that from a Widget when you click on the Dashboard too. It's possible to create your own widgets too.

Using Widgets In Dashboard

Dashboard is always open, really, even if you don't see it. The pellucid look of it really gives it an ethereal feel: A creeping ghost that is there but can't be seen, only felt. Some Mac users complain because these little apps suck a lot of power—namely, your RAM is used from your Real Memory. In layman's terms, even when you're not using Dashboard, it's still using a lot of your computer's power. There are ways to "shut off" dashboard, too, but we won't get into that here.

There are a couple ways to get Dashboard's Widgets to appear on the forefront of your screen. There is a Dashboard Icon on your Dock where you can access the screen by clicking that Icon. There is an easier way if your hands are busy with Quick Keys on the keyboard. Use the F12 key to get Dashboard to fade onto your screen (and off) when you need it.

You don't have to keep the Widgets where they are already placed. This is a simple default setting. Move the widgets, add or delete them at your whim. You drag the Widgets like you would any other folder or icon on the desktop. To see all the Widgets pre-loaded with Leopard, you'll have to press the plus sign (+) in the left-lower corner of the screen after Dashboard is turned ON (screen). To add one, click it from the bottom. If you'd like to see all the Widgets pre-made for Dashboard, go _here_.

In order to get a Widget to go away from your main dashboard screen, you'll want to click the (X) that appears next to it (after clicking the (+) button to the bottom-left). Pushing this lets you add (and take away) Widgets that you'll use most. To make it go away, and make it aesthetically pleasing, push the (+) again. The screen will drop back down to the normal view mode.

Principal Widgets Explained

Here are some basic explanations of some of the Widgets from the Mac Dashboard Support web pages:

Widget Manager—This widget manages other widgets. Uncheck Widgets that you don't want to use anymore and it will hide and disable them. You can keep check of all your available widgets from here.

Address Book—This widget feeds off Address Book proper, enabling you to look up a person's email address, phone number, and mailing address quickly. Just start typing a name in the search field, or click the arrow buttons to step through all entries.

Business—The Business widget is a great directory of local businesses and substitute for your yellow pages. Just type a business name or category (like "pizza") in the search field, and view your results in the expanded window. To change the local city, click the "i" button; enter a city, state, or zip code; and click Done.

Calculator—This electronic version works just like its real-world counterpart, letting you add, subtract, multiply, and divide numbers without thought. You can enter numbers by clicking the buttons or pressing the numeric keys on your keyboard.

Dictionary—Get word definitions, synonyms, and antonyms for any English language word you type in the search field. And because the dictionary is built into Leopard, you don't need an Internet connection to get this information.

ESPN—For sports fans, this widget displays the latest scores and news for your favorite baseball, basketball, football, and hockey teams. Just click the "i" button in the upperright corner and choose a sport from the pop-up menu. When finished, click "News" to view the latest news feeds from ESPN or "Scores" to see how well your team is faring.

Flight Tracker—View the flight paths of practically any upcoming or in-progress flight around the world. Just choose an airline, departure city, and arrival city from the pop-up menus (or enter the information in the fields), click Find Flights, select the flight in the results, and click Track Flight.

Google—When you need information fast, just type what you're looking for into this widget to make Google scour the Internet on your command. Your default web browser will automatically open to display the search results.

iCal—This widget allows you to view the current day and date in a small calendar, as well as view days and dates in the future and past. Just click the up or down arrow buttons to jump through the calendar by month.

iTunes—This widget allows you to control iTunes playback (iTunes must be open for this to work). You can use the widget controls to play, pause, and skip forward and backward through songs in your iTunes Library or a playlist, or listen to Internet radio. You can even control volume with a twist of the outer dial.

Movies—Heading out to enjoy a movie? Use this widget to look up information about the latest releases and find show times at local theaters. Not sure if you would enjoy the movie? Watch movie trailers right in Dashboard, then click to buy tickets.

People—Feeling out of touch with friends and family? Don't use that old excuse of losing their phone numbers. Look them up with this widget, which can look up residential phone numbers by area. Just enter a first name, last name, and a city and state or zip code.

Ski Report—Find out the current weather and snow conditions at popular skiing locations across the country and head for the hills. Just click the "i" button in the bottom-right corner and type the name of a resort to get the current conditions, including the new snowfall, base depth, and temperature.

Stickies—Just like the paper version but for your Mac. Just type notes right on the Stickies pad. To change the paper color and font, click the "i" button in the bottom-right corner. Then select a paper color, choose a font from the Font pop-up menu, choose a font size from the other pop-up menu, and click Done.

Stocks—This widget lets you track your favorite stocks (with up to a 20-minute delay). To enter a company, click the "i" button in the bottom-right corner, type the company's name or ticker symbol in the field, and click Done. To get an overview of your stock's performance, click the company symbol to view a graph that shows the highs and lows over a user-selectable timeframe.

Tile Game—You probably remember this one as a kid; the goal of the game is to rearrange all the tiles so that they form a picture. Just click the widget to make it start scrambling the tiles. Click it again to make it stop. To rearrange tiles, click a tile that borders the empty space to move it in its place, and continue in this manner until you see the picture again.

Translation—For those times when you can't decipher a foreign language phrase, or you need to translate one of your own into another language, this widget comes in handy. Just choose the language that you want to translate from and to using the pop-up menus, and type the word or phrase in the text box below "Translate from." C'est facile!

Unit Converter—If you need to convert weights, measurements, temperatures, speeds, currency, volume, and other items, this widget will do the job. Just choose a unit category from the Convert pop-up menu, choose a unit that you want converted from the bottomleft pop-up menu, choose the unit that you want it converted to in the bottom-right popup menu, and enter a value in the left field to view the conversion to its right.

Weather—Be prepared wherever you may roam. The Weather widget displays the current weather conditions for the city of your choice in thermal terms (high, low, and current temperatures) and in current graphical conditions too. Click on the widget for a 5-day forecast. To change the city, click the "i" button; enter a city, state, or zip code; and click Done.

Web Clip—Say you check part of a particular website pretty often. Why not turn it into a widget? In Safari, click the Web Clip icon and select the part of the page you want to turn into a widget. Click Add and Safari launches your brand-new widget in Dashboard. From there you can customize it with a selection of themes. Your new web clip widget is always live, acting just like the website it was clipped from.

World Clock—The World Clock widget displays the local time for many cities around the world. Open multiple windows to keep track of different time zones. To change the city, click the "i" button, choose a continent from the Continent pop-up menu, choose a city from the City pop-up menu, and click Done.

Ch. 8 Chapter Eight: From Customize To Corners

The Personalized Apple

Making Your Mac: Know it To Own It

As spoken about in previous chapters, Apple's creation of the Mac entails customization. In other words, Apple comes with a universal running system pre-installed. Unless you bought your new-to-you Mac from eBay, then you've probably got the newest version of Leopard (pre-) installed. In any case, like your car, house, office or cubicle, you've formulated a reflective version of your self, seen through the things you own. Unlike the bigwigs atop the PC software world (Micro-something), Apple truly tries to help you help your Mac fit you better.

If you want to either simply show off your Mac or clearly know its in-and-outs, here are some cooler things on top of what is already cool—doesn't that make it HOT? From here on out, you'll know not only some chill assets, but you'll learn about Hot Corners, Keyboard shortcuts and overall customization.

Cool Mac Forged Hot

As mentioned, your Mac can do some jaw-dropping tricks. Some of these—maybe subsidiary—shortcuts are merely for your customization enjoyment while others escalate and encourage work rate and fecundity. It's always nice to have your heart race at the entertainment of it all. Be that as it may, here are some of the marginal yet momentous maneuvers making a Mac Your Mac.

Dictionary Defined

One of the neatest features of using Leopard—or any 10.4 OS X for that matter—is the dictionary or thesaurus window. Say you're in Safari, reading the news about the economy or technology. You come across a word you've never seen before: "snafu," for example. If you'd like to see the dictionary meaning of the word, it's quite simple. Here's how:

Don't highlight, but just place your mouse cursor over the word. Press and depress Ctrl + Cmd + D. The word "snafu" will then become highlighted. Below the highlighted tablike box, you'll see whether the word is a verb, noun, adjective or adverb. Below that, you'll see numbered definitions in a list format.

In the very left hand corner of the highlighted tab box, you'll see a scroll down option menu. If you'd like the thesaurus, you can check this option (choose Oxford Thesaurus). If you press more… in the right hand bottom corner of the same box, the Mac Dictionary Application will open. From here, you'll have the definition in its entirety, or you can type in other words for a quick lookup and denotation. By the way, this Dictionary only works on Applications Mac-based (Cocoa: Safari, Mail, MacJournal, TextEdit, Comic Life, iWeb and so forth.)

Text Talking

If you're working alone, you can have your Mac talk to you, say what you want it to say, or read text. Though the feature is perhaps not as indispensable as the Dictionary function, you can still get some good uses. It's handy if you're giving a presentation and want your Mac to read to the audience; if you'd like to hear rather than read some text document; or, for those that may not be able to talk normally due to a handicap or dental operation gone awry.

You should first open or launch *Terminal*. If you can't find it, you can do so by using Spotlight, searching for *Terminal* and clicking it open from there. A white box will appear on your screen. Your last login will show up with the date and time. If you'd like your Mac to tell you how great you are, type, "say you are such a great person _____ " for example (without quotes). Your computer will likely "ahem" and then say it.

If you'd like *Terminal* to read you a text document (.txt document), you must type "say – f" plus the name of the file, presentation.txt, for example (say –f presentation.txt).

Slow Significance

If you'd like to slow things down on your Mac, again for show more than for service, you can make things happen in slow motion. When Steve Jobs first showed this, the audience cheered. If you'd like to get the same effects, then all you have to do is hold down the *Shift* key when you minimize, close applications or bring up *Dashboard*.

If you've got an Application opened, such as Safari, here's how to slow it down too: Hold down the Shift key as mentioned earlier. Press the yellow circle button in the left, top corner of the window with your mouse. When you do so, the Safari window will slow down four or five times. Macs are so hot you have to slow it down so others will see to believe.

Seize Snapshots

By far, one of the coolest schemes you can do is take a picture of anything, anytime, anywhere with your Mac. There are several ways— and more reasons—to do this. Here are three of the unique ways to take a picture (a screenshot [and more] if you will) of any webpage, picture, application, movie or document.

- If you'd like to take a picture of a webpage in its entirety, then you'll have to have the webpage open and simultaneously press **Ctrl + Shift + 3**. You'll hear a snapshot camera noise. If you save downloads to your desktop, then you'll see the picture file end in .png. You can change this to .jpeg simply by clicking on the file, type in the change to .jpeg, and click *use .jpg* when the

"Are you sure…" box appears.

- If you'd like to take a picture of just part of a webpage, movie or any running application, then you'll have to press **Ctrl + Shift + 4**. This will make your cursor turn to cross hairs. To capture the image, simply hold down the mouse button and frame the image within the gray-ish shaded box. The picture will then be taken. When you open it, your Mac will automatically open *Preview* in order to show the "picture" to you.
- Lastly, you can capture any active running application, like in Safari. This time, press and depress Ctrl + Shift + 4 again plus the spacebar. The cross hairs will morph into a camera. The background will turn blue. When you click the mouse, the active window picture will be captured. You can copy all this to your clipboard by pressing **Shift + Ctrl + Command + 4**.

As mentioned, your files will be saved as .png files. It is possible to change this from the get-go rather than wait till the image is saved to your desktop. To do so, open Terminal and type this:

defaults write com.apple.screencapture type png

To change from png, type whatever you'd like the picture to be saved as: png, PDF, tiff or jpeg. You'll have to log out and back in for this change to start.

Zenith Zooming

Most of us Mac users know we can make our screen text bigger by pressing **Command** plus the + sign and text smaller **Command** plus the – sign. If you're using *Safari* and reading the news online, then make the text bigger by using this option.

If, however, you'd just like to zoom in—magnifying style—then it's equally as painless. All you have to do is press **Ctrl** and use two fingers to drag up and down on the touchpad. You can use the "pinch" method or the simple "scroll" method—moving two fingers up and down (e.g. north to south) to get the zoom effect. And things just get better from here!

Summon Spotlight

The quickest way to open and close Spotlight is to use the keyboard shortcut: **Cmd + Spacebar**. Spotlight helps you find any number of files starting with top hits, Applications, Preferences, documents, folders, PDF documents, music, movies, presentation and more.

One of the easiest ways to find and open an *Application* is to open it from *Spotlight,* rather than going into your *Finder,* for instance. In *System Preferences,* under the *Personal* row, you can click on *Spotlight* to customize it. You might think about placing Applications in the Top Hits section of Spotlight as to make it quicker to open hard-to find Applications. Perchance this option is useful for Applications you sometimes use, and don't want clogging your dock.

Hidden Hues

This next customization tip is more of a trick rather than a tip, per se. What you'll do here simply invert the colors of your computer screen. What it really looks like, though, is a color-negative of a picture of your screen. This could be a fun, cruel joke to play on your friends or fellow Mac lovers.

What you have to do is simple. Simply press **Ctrl** + **Option** + **Cmd** + **8**. This single click command will have the colors of your computer screen flipped. Press the same sequence again to undo the inversion.

Skimming Searches

Most PCs make it really difficult to change from one running application to another. Unfortunately, the same is true with Mac in some instances. There are other ways, but here's a nifty trick to help save you time plus the frustration of searching for all those documents running in one Application.

The first way we in the Mac world are taught to change from one running Application to another is to use the **Cmd** + **tab** key. This brings up inflated icons of the Applications. Though colorful and fun, this function is also limited to just opening the Application itself with no choice into getting at individual documents quickly. If you've got 10 individual Pages or Word documents open, for example, the **Cmd** + **tab** key will only open "Pages" or "Word." Now, though, there's an easy way to sift through those 10 documents more quickly.

After opening the running Application you'd like, you can search through the documents by pressing the **Cmd** + ~. This allows you to skim through them at warp speed. If only one document is open, for example, this quick key function doesn't do anything. If you do the same thing in Firefox or Safari, you can zip through these web windows just as quickly. Few people know this little trick.

Screen Sections

There are a ton more quick keys than abovementioned (and we'll get into more of those later), but what if you could simply do things with a wave of your mouse. Instead of pressing F11 to clear your screen or F12 to bring up Dashboard, you can do the same with your mouse or from the touchpad of your laptop. What you'll have to do is set each or some corners of your screen as Hot Corners or *Active Screen Corners*. This means that when your cursor is in the upper-left hand corner of the screen, for example, your screen will clear (like pressing F11). Another wave of the mouse brings the Applications to the forefront.

In order to do this, go into the Silver (or blue) half-bitten apple in the upper left hand corner of your screen. Now, open *System Preferences*. In Leopard, you'll select the *Expose & Spaces* icon (fourth one over). (In Tiger, it's the second icon reading Dashboard & Expose.) Now, you'll have the option to set each or just one or two Active Screen Corners. You can customize this to do any number of the F# options. You can set the All Windows, Desktop, Dashboard and Application Windows to activate when you sweep over any of your screen's four corners.

Varying Volume

The F4 and F5 keys above may seem like a waste of space as it seems that its only objective is to decrease or increase (respectively) the volume. Well, that is pretty much it, but you can also open the Sound in System Preferences window from them. You can choose an alert sound, adjust the alert volume or change the output and input of an external mic and/or speakers. In order to open the window, press **Option + F4** or F5.

Gift of Grab

The Grab Application is an almost forgotten Mac application. The invention of the screenshot spoken about above has seemingly replaced this cool Mac feature. Grab actually allows you to do a couple effects differently than screenshots. Here's what and how:

You can actually take a timed screenshot with Grab. The easiest way to go about grabbing a screenshot is to firstly open Grab. (Go to Spotlight [**Cmd + spacebar**] and type Grab). If you press **Cmd + Shift + Z**, the *Timed Screen Grab* box appears. After you press *Start Timer*, you'll have 10 seconds before a screenshot is taken. Another neat option is the ability to change the pointer style. If you go into Grab and then *Preferences*, you'll be given seven or eight pointer options to choose from.

Smooth Move

Often when we open a webpage, we scroll down but the chop-a-block style is very rigid and really not as smooth as the rest of the Mac functions. Available in Tiger and Leopard, though, is an action called Smooth Scrolling. Using this option allows you the user to scroll through a document or longer webpage without the stringent or ironclad-ness as before. It's very easy.

Open up *System Preferences*. Under the *Personal* section, click on *Appearance*. Here, you'll see the option to "Use Smooth Scrolling" in the second partition. Click on it to enable smoother movements or untick it to disable and revert back to the "old" style.

*Don't forget that with the click of the spacebar while on a webpage, you can scroll through longer news reports, blogs or webpages more easily. With the smooth scrolling ticked and on, you'll more easily see where you left off in your last line of reading.

Ch. 9 Chapter Nine: From Startup To Shutdown

The Expeditious Apple

Shortcut Keys & Quicker Commands

The customization discussed in chapter eight will help with the efficiency at which you complete your work. The whole idea behind customization is to make your Mac more user-friendly and personable. Now, though, it's time to learn about Mac's shortcut keys.

The shortcut keys empower you to zip through applications, windows, commands, and editing that would otherwise make your mouse-finger fatigue. Unlike customization of your Mac, the shortcut keys are always the same for every Mac. It's your choice to learn and implement them. It's really not a matter of memorization but more precisely using the ones that help you most.

Shortcut Hot Keys

Below is the list of shortcut keys and a description of what those keys will do within the opened or running window. Though a thorough account of the shortcut keys is included here, there may be more available on the Mac Support WebPages. Rather than include a boxy table outlining the keystrokes, this orderly bullet point list will provide you with an easy-to-read and functioning outline of Mac's shortcuts. (Some shortcut keystrokes only work in Leopard while others only work in former OS X systems. Most work with both.) You'll find Shortcut Keys below under the following Apple themes:

o Finder window
   o Startup
o Applications
   o Dock
o Shutdown
   o Spaces
o Mouse keys
   o Screenshots
o Menu
   o Editing
o Mac Help

Shortcut Keys in Finder

Finder lets you see everything on your Mac in a concise order. You can even choose the style: icon, list and column view. From the Finder, you should be able to find anything on your Mac. You can easily get to the Finder by clicking on the smiley Mac boxhead located in your dock—it's usually the first icon. Once open, you'll notice a sidebar to the left. When you click on one of the left icons, you can then see the folder's contents to the right.

- Cmd + J – Opens view options
- Cmd + K – Connects you to server dialogue box
- Cmd + F – Find dialogue box
- Cmd + Shift + Delete – Empty trash (with warning)
- Cmd + Shift + Delete + Option – Empty Trash (without warning)
- Cmd + Down Arrow – Takes you to selected folder
- Cmd + Up Arrow – Takes you to the parent folder
- Cmd + [- Takes you back
- Cmd +] – Takes you forward
- Cmd + C, Cmd + V – Copy then paste selected item
- Cmd + D – Copies selected

54

- Cmd + O – Opens selected
- Cmd + Z – Undoes last action
- Cmd + 1 (or 2,3,4) – Changes List view to Icon view, for example
- Cmd + Shift + C (H, I, A, F) – Goes to iDisk, Applications, Favorites etc
- Cmd + W – Closes running window
- Cmd + Option + W – Close all windows

Shortcut Keys For Startup

Mac usually starts up without any sort of problems. All you see is the screen come on and then after a timely boot up, you choose your user name and type in your password. There are some things you can do when your computer starts up, however, that will give you that behind the scenes command post into your computer. Here are some shortcut keys when you first start up your Mac.

- Cmd + S – single user mode
- Cmd + T – FireWire disk mode
- Cmd + C – Starts CD with system folder
- Cmd + X - Mac OS Start up
- Hold Shift – Starts in Safe Boot mode

Shortcut Keys For Applications

The Applications on your Mac are all those icons found under the Applications menu. To get to the Applications folder, click on Finder and on the left side click on Applications. Once you do, you'll be able to scroll down through all the Applications on your computer. Once you have Applications open—say Safari, iCal, iTunes, Mail—you can then use the following quick key commands to switch through them and do all sorts of things.

- Cmd + Tab – Switch between two running Applications quickly
- Cmd + Tab – Hold Cmd and press Tab to switch through chosen Applications
- Cmd + ~ - Quickly switch between Applications (& go left after Cmd + Tab)
- Cmd + Q – Quit a running Application (after Cmd + Tab)
- Cmd + H – Hides running Applications (after Cmd + Tab)
- Cmd + Esc – Cancels out of the Cmd + Tab Application switcher

Shortcut Keys For Dock

Like the dock you used to fish safely from as a kid keeps you above the water, so too the Mac Dock keeps you safely on top of your most-used Mac Applications. The Dock is one of the neatest functions setting your Mac apart from the run-of-the-mill PC. With it, there's no out-of-place icons floating on your screen nor is there a need to sift through Programs before you start an Application. Below you'll find some useful shortcut keys to help you utilize your Mac's Dock.

- Cmd + Click (on Dock icon) – Quickly takes you to the item in the Finder
- Cntrl (hold) + shift – Turn magnification on/off in Dock
- Shift (hold over divider) – Move the dock to left, right, and bottom
- Drag file over App icon and hold Cmd + Option – The file will open in that App
- Cmd + Option (while click on App icon) – Hides all other running Applications
- Cmd + Drag Icon – Move the Application to another hard drive location
- Option + Cmd + D – Hides the Dock

Shortcut Keys For Shutdown

Sometimes you have to step away from your computer—from running tight-legged to the bathroom to saving the pot from boiling over. Rather than drag your mouse or keypad finger to the little blue or gray apple in the menu bar and scroll down to Sleep, Restart or Shutdown, there are faster ways to shutting down your Mac. Make sure you are constantly saving your work. Also, take fare warning that these shortcut keys will only offer the box confirmation half the time.

- Ctrl + Shift + Eject – Will put your display asleep
- Ctrl + Eject – Brings up box confirmation: restart, sleep, cancel or shutdown
- Cmd + Opt + Eject – Puts your computer to sleep (w/o box confirmation)
- Cmd + Opt + Ctrl + Eject – Will shutdown your computer (w/o box confirmation)

Shortcut Keys for Spaces

Spaces is the program in Leopard that allows you to organize your screen's muddle into a classy marshal of spaces. Easier put,

Spaces allows you to take all those running Applications and then reorganize windows—think of them as shelves or rooms or boxes—by Application. Spaces makes finding those Applications easier and quicker with its bird's-eye view (BEV). Add shortcut keys and you'll be moving through your work at time twisting speeds.

- F8 – Gives you the BEV of running Applications (Hint: Make a hot corner with Exposé so you aren't always reaching up for the F8 key.)
- Cmd + Drag (with mouse or finger) – doing this in the BEV enables you to move running Applications into different windows
- Ctrl + Arrow Keys – Move to adjacent Spaces while in BEVing
- F8 then press C – Puts the Spaces windows into one workspace (to restore, press C again)

Shortcut Keys for Mouse Keys

If you'd like to make your keyboard or number keypad work like your mouse—say it died or you forgot it or dropped it—you can do so through the Universal Access window. Open Universal Access and click on the Mouse & Trackpad tab. If you'd like your keypad to "be" your mouse, then you have to also turn on the Fn key (or num lock [often F6]). You can even set it up so that when you press the Option key five times, the mouse keys will automatically start.

- 8 – Moves your mouse up
- 2 – Moves your mouse down
- 4 - Moves your mouse left
- 6 Moves your mouse right
- 1,3,7,9 - Moves your mouse diagonally
- 5 – Mouse click
- 0 – Mouse button "hold"
- . – Mouse button "release"

Shortcut Keys For Screenshots

Though we spoke of the screenshot option in previous chapters, we'll go over them again here—that's how important they are. As one of the neat-o functions of your Mac, and once you start to use them, these shortcut keys will keep your more organized, working faster than ever. Unless you change the file extension, it will automatically show up as a .png.

- Cmd + Shift + 3 – Screenshot of entire screen
- Cmd + Shift + 4 – Use crosshairs to drag over and select frame

- Cmd + Shift + 4 + Spacebar – Brings up camera icon for image capture
- Hold Ctrl – Enables you to copy the screenshot onto the clipboard

Shortcut Keys For Menu

At the top of every Mac, no matter the OS X version, you'll find the ubiquitous Menu bar. On the left, are the words File, Edit, View, Go, Window and Help. To the right, you'll find the icons for Spaces, Bluetooth, Internet, Time Machine and the date and time (and more). To see which Application, if any, is running, you can simply read the Name to the right of the apple. If it says Pages, for instance, then you know that the running Application is Pages. If you'd like to get back to the Apple Menu Bar, you can click on the desktop.

- Shift + Cmd + Q – Log Out of Your Username
- Shift + Option + Cmd + Q – Log out Quickly (no box confirmation)
- Shift + Cmd + Delete – Empties Trash (with box confirmation)
- Cmd + Alt + Space – Brings up Spotlight Guide
- Cmd + H – Hides running Applications
- Cmd + I – Get Info for file
- Cmd + M – Minimize running Application to Dock
- Cmd + Option + M – Minimize all running windows of same App to Dock
- Cmd + Option + H – Hides all windows except one working on
- Ctrl + Eject – Shutdown, sleep or restart
- Cmd + , - Open Preferences for running Application window
- Cmd + Option + Esc – Force Quit Application

Shortcut Keys for Editing

When you're working on a document in Pages, Numbers, Word or Keynotes (and many other Applications), you'll need shortcut keys to make your work run more smoothly. Whether moving around text, some screenshot or .jpeg, be sure to use these shortcut keys. You'll probably use these more than any others discussed in this chapter if you are an artists, writer, designer or work with images and/or text often.

- Cmd + Z – Undo last move (un-bold, delete paste, undo hyperlink etc)
- Cmd + A – Select All (highlight)
- Cmd + C – Copy
- Cmd + V – Paste

- Cmd + X – Cut/Remove highlighted (can re-paste later)
- Cmd + N – New document (or window in Safari or other browser)
- Cmd + T – New Tab Window (in Safari or other browser or Applications)
- Cmd + S – Saves work
- Cmd + B – Bold highlighted or bold text thereafter
- Cmd + I – Italicize highlighted or italics text thereafter
- Cmd + U – Underlines highlighted or underlines text thereafter
- Cmd + Right Arrow – Takes cursor to end of the line
- Cmd + Left Arrow – Takes cursor to the beginning of line
- Cmd + Down Arrow – Goes to end of text (in document, i.e.)
- Cmd + Up Arrow – Goes to beginning of text
- Option + Right Arrow – Goes to end of next word
- Option + Left Arrow – Goes to beginning of previous word

*Use the Shift Key and highlight with the above cursor commands.

*The following only works only in some running Applications
- Cmd + Shift + C- Brings up Color palette
- Cmd + T – Brings up Font palette
- Cmd + { (hold Shift to make { on the [key) – Aligns cursor/ selected left
- Cmd + } (hold Shift to make } on the] key) – Aligns cursor/ selected right
- Cmd + | (hold Shift to make | on the \ key) – Aligns selected to center
- Cmd + ; - Checks Spelling

Shortcut Key for Mac OS Help

With the Mac OS Help Window, you can do so much to help you with questions, problems or just inquiries that you may have about you Mac. You can even connect to the Apple.com website from here. If you got Tiger, then you'll have access to What's New, Features, Discovering Your Mac, and the Top Customer Issues. If you're using Leopard, however, by using the following shortcut key command, you'll bring up a Help Menu when on the desktop. You'll simply type in the keyword or subject you're after on the box (a lot like Spotlight).

- Cmd + Shift + ? – Brings up Mac OS Help

My Mac Shortcut Keys

Below, pencil in your favorite shortcut keys you'd like to start using with your Mac. Instead of highlighting them from above (and then having to flip through the pages), write them in here for quicker reference; then, post it in your office for quicker learning. Once you get the hang of them, you can then disregard this little cheat sheet.

Ch. 10 Chapter Ten: From System To Preferences

The Preferred Apple

System Preferences… & What it means

Apple's Mac is all about you, the user. Whenever possible, Apple tries to think of neat ways to make 'A' Mac computer 'Your' Mac computer. Nowhere else in the corporate computer world will you find such efforts to not only please customers but help them really feel that they are in total control of how their machine operates.

In the last chapter we talked about working with your Mac's shortcut keys. In the same light, this chapter explains what your System Preferences… is, what it does and some things you can do to configure everything from screen resolution, sound to keyboard and mouse controls. We've already spoken, too, about the Applications and what each of these can do for you.

Now, it's time to get started on each of the preferences and what each icon under the Personal, Hardware, Internet & Network and System (& Other) does for you. In order to open the *System Preferences…* you must go up to the silver once-bitten apple at the top of the menu bar and scroll down to *System Preferences…*to get started.

System Preferences: The Personal Preference

Appearance

In the newest OS for Mac, some things have gotten incredibly better and faster and more user-friendly, while other choices have, well, remained the same. Whether it is Apple's intention to be conservative in some preferences—such as Appearance—or simply to leave alone what is good, we users may not see many changes to some preferences as long as we do not work for Apple's design team. At any rate, the Appearance preference is practically the same from Tiger to Leopard.

With *System Preferences…* open, you'll see the four categories mentioned in the introduction. Under the Personal category, you'll click on Appearance. From here you can:

- Select the color for the look of your windows, panes, menus and buttons
- Change the highlight color when you run your cursor over text to be highlighted
- Change your scroll arrow location: either together or separated on opposite ends
- Change how the scroll bar works: from going to the next page, to going to the location you click, and whether or not you want smooth scrolling on/off
- Set the number of most recent items displayed (makes recent items quicker to open: from 5 to 50) for Applications, Documents and Servers
- Set your font smooth over and style: from Automatic to Standard to Light and Strong
- Change whether font smoothing is on/off for a specific font size
- Click on the question mark in any *System Preference...* preference pane to search for answers to that particular preference

Desktop & Screensaver

The Desktop & Screensaver preferences, like that of Appearance, have really remained the same. Yes, this makes it easier to remember from previous OS, but doesn't really give users any newer inclinations to think Apple wants change. As we're not here to judge, this preference is one of the easiest to use. When you click on Desktop & Screensaver you can:

- (Now in Leopard) Choose to turn on/off the Translucent Menu bar,
- Add or take away folders
- Have desktop pictures appear in a random order
- Change the picture(s)—from seconds to hours
- Choose your desktop picture from any Apple file
- (Within Screensaver) Choose a screensaver
- Choose to make your screensavers appear randomly
- Turn the clock on or off
- Change the display of the screensaver: fade, turning frames (collage) or mosaic panels
- Change the time at which your screensaver begins (with the scroll button)

- Select or change the Energy Saver preference
- Select options for how to present the screensaver: random, cross-fade, zoom, crop and centered
- Access *Hot Corners*…to make screensaver come up at your quick command
- Test the screensaver to see if you like the setup
- Preview the screensaver on the small preview screen

Dock

With Leopard's Dock, as we've spoken about in several preceding chapters, countless updates (shall we say improvements) have taken place. From the Dock's design to layout to fashion—while holding on to tradition—have given us a design most Mac users are happy with. As to avoid critique or humdrum review of the preference itself (it's the same too!), here is what you can do when you click on the Dock icon in System Preferences:

- Change the size of the dock (with scroll tab)
- Turn on/off magnification
- Change how small or large the magnification of the Dock's icons become
- Change the positioning of the Dock (Yes: left, bottom, right)
- Choose which effect you'd like to minimize using: Genie and Scale Effect
- Animate the opening of Applications when you click on them (this will also show the bounce feature when an Application needs your immediate attention)
- And, choose to show or hide the Dock no matter where you position it (good for people who want their entire screen "free"; not good if you have twenty icons)

Exposé & Spaces

In the older OS X running systems, the preference icons were adjoined with Dashboard & Exposé together. Dashboard has been removed from the System Preferences icons entirely to now show Exposé & Spaces together (where you now have the Dashboard preference at the bottom of the Exposé preference window). Here's what you can choose to do under the Exposé & Spaces preference:

- (Exposé) Make active screen corners for some or all four corners of your screen
- Using the screen corners, you can make each one open *All Windows, Application Windows, Desktop, Dashboard, Spaces,*

Start and Disable, Sleep and *Off*
- With Exposé, you can quickly access any open and running window: assign any of the F# keys or a multitude of other keys like command, Alt and Ctrl
- Hide or show the Dashboard; Choose F# Key or others to activate Dashboard; and, choose to use (or not) the Mouse Buttons
- (Spaces) Tick to Enable (or not) the Spaces option: Lets you organize your running Applications into groups of organized windows
- Tick to show Spaces in the Menu bar
- Add or take away rows and columns
- Add an Application
- Add and choose a Space
- Apply keyboard and mouse shortcuts (default F8); choose how you navigate through the spaces (when you use the bird's eye view)

International

If you compare Tiger OS with Leopard OS, the interface for the International pane is exactly the same. Though they may be identical in appearance, however, Leopard's International preference is more powerful. With the necessity to communicate more with your global neighbors, Leopard uses Spotlight, for example, to improve character, dictionary and indexing of German, Thai and Chinese languages. There are even fifteen more keyboard layouts, from Tibetan, Kasakh to Persian. You'll find character palettes for several other languages too. Here's what you can do in the three—Language, Formats and Input Menu—tabs under the *International* preference.

- (Language tab) Choose anything from English, Italiano to Polski and Korean.
- You can drag an drop your language preference
- Or, you can click the "Edit List" button to tick whether you want the language to even be a choice or not
- Select or change the order you'd like the languages to be sorted
- Choose the way the words break—standard, US English or Japanese
- (Formats tab) Choose your region and tick to show them all or not
- Customize (rearrange) the way your dates appear by drag and drop (click "Customize…" button)
- The dates can appear by short, medium, long or full (1/10/08 versus January 10th, 2008, for example)

- Under the Times bar, you can also choose how your time appears (7:10 pm versus 7:10:09: PM: GMT + 02:00, for example)
- Under the Numbers bar, you can choose Metric or US measurements
- You can also pick which currency to use as default—from Afgani to the Czech Koruna to the US Dollar
- (Input Menu) Turn On/Off the character Palettes
- Letter prediction for Japanese characters (and some other languages)
- See the Name, Input Type and Script (lettering/alphabet style) in the row

Security

Anytime security is an issue on Mac, you can bet that it's there for reason. On no other machine will you have this many security options. With Leopard, specifically, there are three new categories to choose from—General, FileVault and Firewall. Each of these tabs at the top give you the chance to really secure or un-secure your Mac. If you don't ever share your computer, keep it at the office and occasionally have some personal information on there, it may be smart to take a gander at some of these new and improved security options.

- (General tab) As always, you can choose to require a password to wake the computer (specific to you as the Master user)
- (For all account users on your computer) Choose to disable the automatic login— necessary especially if the computer is shared or partitioned
- The System Preferences… really allows users to get at the guts. So, you can tick a box to make any changes to passwords. No changes can ever take place if the user doesn't know the original Master Password
- Auto log out of inactive users: 1 min to 999 min
- Use secure virtual memory—Allows you to use more memory and store more info because the computer writes the info differently. If someone wants to recover information that you wanted gone, for example, turning the virtual memory ON will make this easier. Keep it Off if you use sensitive data
- You can disable the infrared remote that came with your computer (Mac Mini, MacBook, etc)
- Make any remote work with your computer by "Pairing" them
- (FileVault tab) Encrypts your computer's contents. It will open/close them when you use them as long as you know the Master

Password
- Set Master Password by following the button's directions (always remember it)
- Turn ON/Off FileVault
- (Firewall tab) Keep your computer "open" to outside connections
- Turn ON/Off the essential services (Internet WiFi, for example)
- Add specific applications with the Advanced... option

Spotlight

Spotlight is that little bloodhound that allows you to practically find anything on your computer. By pushing the Cmd + Spacebar, the Spotlight will appear in the top-right of your screen. The Spotlight preference, on the other hand, allows you to change the innerworkings of Spotlight by simply dragging and dropping your computer's categories as you'd like them to appear. So, you can:

- Change the order in which your computer's categories show up when you search for things with Spotlight
- You won't be able to delete the "category" but you can put it last on the list (number 14) under the Search Results tab; you can un-tick the category to keep it from showing up entirely when you perform a Spotlight search too
- Change the shortcut key to any of the F# options
- Change which keys operate the Spotlight Menu and Window
- (Privacy) Keeps certain choice files, documents or folders from appearing when a search is performed in Spotlight
- drag and drop the files—pictures, documents, passwords, media and the like— into the list window; you can also add or remove the files with the + and – buttons
- Again, you can change the shortcut keys under the Private tab too

System Preferences: The *Hardware* Preference

Bluetooth

You may not even know what Bluetooth is or care to know. The thing is that Bluetooth technology is the predecessor of what is happening big in the wireless world. With Bluetooth, you can connect handheld devices (the goal of our techno-centric world), mobile phones, computers, keyboards or the Mighty Mouse and other devices to your computer—sometimes called pairing or a.k.a. "talking to each other." The devices connect without the needs for wires and uses a short-range technology to connect wirelessly together, up to around 10 metes or 30-some feet apart. With the Bluetooth preference, you can:

- Turn Bluetooth ON/Off
- Turn Discoverable ON/Off
- Discoverable On allows your computer to "think" for itself in the search of closeby technology devices, signals or 3rd party devices
- Discoverable allows the computer to self-scan
- Set up New Devices, such as mice, keyboards, printers or other devices automatically
- Open up Bluetooth setup assistant to help your computer "find" the device if it doesn't do so automatically through Discoverable (requires a Restart)
- Let's those other synchronized devices to awake your computer
- Warns you about incoming audio connections
- Share the Internet with your computer
- Tick to show or not show Bluetooth in the menu bar
- Add or remove devices from the list with the + and - buttons
- Shut off Bluetooth when you don't need it as it uses a lot of battery power

CDs & DVDs

As long as you don't have the enticing Mac Air, this section will pertain to you. If you've ever wondered how your computer knows (or doesn't) what to do when you put in a CD or DVD, then this section will show you. It's here that you can change which Application or Program opens when your Mac recognizes a disk has been inserted. If you've got one DVD player you like over another and get tired of having DVD Player (the Mac one, for example) open, then here's where you have the power to change how your Mac operates.

- If you put a blank disk into your computer, you'll probably want your Mac to ask you what to do (select this)
- If you want it to always run a certain Application, then choose Open another application... and choose which one you'd like to make the default blank CD program (you can choose iTunes for instance)
- You'll have the same choices if you insert a blank DVD
- (Music CD) Choose which application you'd like to always be the default player
- (Picture CD) Choose an existing application you may have installed

- Choose another Application (Kodak, or the like)
- Run Script allows you to choose a document from your computer's Hard drive
- (Video DVD) By default, start DVD Player (Mac version)
- Or, you can change this by choosing to use another application
- With all of these, you can choose to ignore the automatic or default settings and do it manually every time you insert a disk

Displays

When you click *Display* under the Hardware row, two tabs give you some serious options. The default settings, mind you, are probably the best. However, if you like to futz with all the (advanced but) micro-settings of your Mac, then here are some things you can do while in this preference.

- (Display tab) The default resolution for Tiger and Leopard is 1280 x 800
- If you'd like to change this, then you have some options, though some will be labeled as "stretched" and others as not
- The resolution can be changed from 640 x 480 (stretched and non-stretched), 800 x 500, 1024 x 768 and so on. Really, the only reason to change these settings is if you work with media or need variations in certain images
- Change the brightness of your computer with the slide bar (same as F1 & F2)
- Change the color selection to the millions, thousands or 256 color
- Choose to have the icon display in the menu bar
- (Color tab) Here, you can change the color profile of your screen and apps
- You can calibrate these manually and choose various colors and tones under the Open profile and Calibrate… buttons

Energy Saver

The Energy Saver preference tries to give you the option to make your computer not only more eco-friendly but also to help you conserve and optimize battery power. Under the *Settings* and *Optimization* pull down menus, you'll see a message telling you the performance of your Mac. If you've got the Power Adapter plugged in, for example, your energy savings will be high (as you're not using the battery). If, however, you're using the battery setting, then the message will tell you how much battery power you have left 56 (in % and time). As you change your Energy Saver settings, this message will tell you how well optimized those specific settings are to your computer. You can:

- Under *Optimization,* you can select Better Battery Life, Normal or Better Performance and Custom
- (Sleep tab) Choose when to put your computer to sleep (up to 3 hrs or never)
- Choose when to put your display to sleep (up to 3 hrs or never)
- If you tick the box that reads "put the hard disk to sleep whenever possible," you may run into trouble when watching a movie as the computer may think it is inactive (un-tick this for movie watching if this occurs)
- You can also schedule a day and time to start up or shutdown your computer
- (Options tab) Choose to dim the display
- Have your computer automatically reduce the screen's brightness (un-tick if watching longer movies)
- Choose to have battery life status up in your menu bar (recommended)

Keyboard & Mouse

Under the Keyboard & Mouse preference, you'll have access to ways to really enhance how your mouse, keyboard, trackpad, shortcuts, and Bluetooth react to you. These options can really make a difference of how fast or slow your computer screen scrolls, how fast or slow your mouse double-clicks and so forth. To really get the full effect here, it's best to open this preference and run some of the tests yourself. Many of the settings have a side-to-side scroll button to make the settings easy to calibrate.

- (Keyboard tab) Change the key repeat rate from slow to fast
- Make keyboard delay long or short (test in text field box)
- (Trackpad tab) Make the tracking speed slow to fast
- Change trackpad gestures: two-finger scrolling, horizontal scrolling and zoom (Zoom= (hold) Ctrl + two fingers [or mouse scroll] with Options to change Shortcut key [see Shortcut Key Chapter])
- Change the double clicking speed (with test field area)
- Change the scrolling speed
- (Mouse tab) Adjust tracking, scrolling, double-click speeds
- Change your primary mouse button to left (default) or right
- Change Zoom shortcut key and tick ON/Off
- (Bluetooth) Name and check battery power of (Bluetooth) mouse and keyboard
- Tick to show status in Menu bar and tick whether you want Bluetooth devices to wake your computer up from sleep

- Choose to set up a new Bluetooth device and pair
- (Keyboard Shortcuts tab) Here, you can change the shortcut keys already preprogrammed for your Mac. However, be sure that if you do, that the keyboard shortcut key is not already a default shortcut for something else
- You can add and take away shortcuts and keys by pressing the + or – button; these will allow you to select from scroll down menu
- You can always change the settings by pressing the button if you don't like a shortcut key that you make

Printer & Fax

What (again and again) makes Mac nice is the ease and accessibility of adding and using external hardware. Printing to a new printer, for instance, from a Windows run PC can be more excruciating than simply writing the information by hand. At any rate, to add or take away a Printer for your Mac is way easy. Instead of having tabs, now this preference is all under one screen, delineated by separate field boxes (with pics!). Here, you can:

- Choose the printer in left hand field box (that you've used before)
- Add/take away printer (if you no longer need one or need to add a new one)
- Open print queue with button (this allows you to delete a print job or adjust the order at which documents print)
- Open options and supplies
- Tick to share or not this computer (this is usually off)
- Scroll down to select default printer if you use it often, such as at home or in your office
- Choose default paper size and change from US Letter to tabloids to different sizes of envelopes (tons of options)

Sound

This is the preference on your Mac where you can really adjust either the internal mic or speakers (input and output volumes) or add and then adjust external devices. If you use Skye or iChat a lot—say in a noisy café or near a busy street—then you can make adjustments that help you and your partner hear each other better.

- Choose an Alert sound and change it to a more, let's say, interesting one
- Tick or un-tick whether or not to play user interface, play feedback, or play front row

- Change output volume and whether to show volume icon in the menu bar or not
- (Output tab) Allows you to balance the chosen speakers and whether to mute the output volume
- (Input tab) calibrate and check internal mic
- Change input (when you speak, for example) and output volume (what you hear)
- Reduce the ambient (outside) noise coming into the mic (for that busy highway or noisy café)**System Preferences: The *Internet & Network* Preference**

.Mac

.Mac is no longer available. *MobileMe* has replaced its services in July of 2008. You can read about *MobileMe* here. The icon for *MobileMe* appears under this row.

Network

Choose the network settings and location here. The Network, for the lay user, is really a good way to get into your Mac to see how well you're Internet connection is doing. You can see the IP address and select to have your Mac do everything Automatically.

- Choose how you want to connect to the Internet, for example, by selecting AirPort, Ethernet, FireWire and so on from the box of icons to the left. You can always add + or take away – with the appropriate buttons.
- Check your status and turn the selected network setting On/Off
- See and change which Network Name your subscribed to (pull down menu)
- Select if you want your computer to ask you before joining a new, perhaps unrecognized, network
- Tick to show or not show the Airport or Bluetooth (and so on) in the upper Menu bar
- Get assistance by pressing *Assist Me…*

QuickTime

QuickTime is a multimedia application first developed by Apple for the Mac OS running systems. It can be used, however, on windows and Linux platforms. With QuickTime, you can finally watch and manipulate real-time movies, sounds, and compressed images. QuickTime is likely the default movie or video box that appears when you download/ streamline a video from another website. QuickTime allows you to:

- Register with your name or organization
- Buy and use QuickTime Pro (if you want external videos to play on your personal website, or if you'd like to do anything to a video aside from watching it
- Play movies automatically or not
- Save the movies or empty the disk cache (recommended)
- Choose the speed of the streaming download
- Choose what sort of delay you'd like once the movie or video clip is streamloading

Sharing

Sharing allows others to access your computer once you tick what can and cannot be accessed by outside parties. Those who want to use your computer's DVD or CD drive remotely will have to be on your network and have permission to do so. Sharing really brings single network experience to a more team and (for lack of better word) shared environment. Mom and Dad would be so proud.

- Turn ON/Off DVD or CD sharing
- Turn On (by ticking) the allowed services from the text field box
- Edit the your computer's local network name: yourname-macbook.local for example

System Preferences: The *System* Preference

Accounts

If you have a Mac computer up and running, then you've already created a user account. If this user account is yours alone, then you are the administrator. You therefore have only one user account and that account is the administrative account—essentially, you decide everything that happens with your Mac—from installing updated software, create, delete and retain other user accounts.

At any rate, whether you have one or five user accounts on your one Mac computer, all the files, media, libraries, and preferences are partitioned from other users, keeping all the things one person does separated from things other users do—as long as everyone has a secret password. Here are some things you can do under the Accounts preference:

- (Password) Select Your ("My"=Admin) or other accounts in the field box to the left

- Add + or take away – user accounts (You'll have to unlock the little golden lock in the left hand corner in order to change Login Options or other user account settings
- Add profile pictures
- Change your password by using the *Change Password...* button
- Change your own user name
- Change your *MobileMe* user name with the *Change...* button
- Open your *Address Book Card* with the *Open...* button and add names and addresses and phone numbers and notes (and edit all those)
- Open *Parental Controls...* from here (see below)
- (Login Items) This is the area that allows you to add and subtract the Applications that automatically open when you (or other users) log in to your computer
- Hide the items that open automatically by ticking the box under "Hide"
- Add an Application to the field box by pressing "add" and your choices will show up (You can change user account information from this pane as well.)

Date & Time

Setting the date and time on your Mac may actually be easier than setting it on your Timex or Rolex (if you be so lucky). The *Date & Time* preference might set automatically by your Mac—don't ask how it knows. Or, if you don't like your Mac thinking for itself, you can change the date and time yourself.

Moreover, you can set it to display in the way you prefer—from the long and drawn out January 1st, 2009 to a simply 1/01/09 display setting. If you'd like to play around with these features because you'd like to actually set the date and time or would like to change the aesthetics of the date/time appearance in the menu bar, here are some things you can do:

- (Date & Time) Tick the "set date & time automatically" (You may have to pick the area of the world you are in.)
- Scroll up and down to change the date
- Choose the date from the Calendar
- Change the time by clicking on the time display box
- Or change the time by holding down the mouse button over the minute or hour hand on the clock display and moving it to the time

- Revert or Save the new time
- Open international preference to set the formats, which allows you to adjust the Language, Formats and Input Menu
- (Time Zone) Move the time zone ray (highlight) over your area of the world
- Then, select the closest city in your time zone from the pull down menu
- (Clock) Allows you to tick to show the date and time in the menu bar (default)
- Tick the way you'd like to view that time (variations)
- Tick the box to announce the time on the hour, half hour or quarter hour
- You can also customize the voice's rate and volume and voice type (male or female with options [Alex is the newest voice])
- Push *Play* to test and *Ok* to set

Parental Control

If parents could just have total control of their kids it would prevent so much…well, trouble, right? Well, with a Mac, you can keep control of your kids with the Parental Control preference. As long as you A.) Don't let your children be the Admin User and B.) Don't give them the password to the Admin User account and C.) Give them their own User Account (that you can monitor as the Admin User).

If your child does not have a User Account, it may be high time to give them one. Just tell them it's to make them feel special and have their "own" computer. In order to make them that special place on the Mac, you'll have to + (add) them as a User and give them a Password (tell them this, of course [but not your Admin User password]). After you've done this, here are some things you can do with the *Parental Control* preference.

- Set the Preferences you would like to Limit: Content, Mail & Chat, Time Limits (YES!), Set allowable dates and times, set Safari to access only certain websites
- Unlock the lock with your password to manipulate other Users' accounts
- After which, you'll have total control of the users by selecting the appropriate name from the list of Users (You'll be taken to the Accounts pane under the Systems preference [See above] to continue)
- Just tick and un-tick the options you'd like to control, from web access to time limits

Software Updates

This preference is a little redundant, but no one at Apple is asking us. So, if you don't like to simply go to the Menu bar at the top and scroll down to *Software Updates*, then you can take the long way round—Opening up *System Preferences…* and then clicking the *Software Updates* preference under the System row. Here are some options you'll have when you'd like to check if there's new security or software updates available from Apple "headquarters."

- (Scheduled Check) Check Now with the button with the same name for the newest software
- See when you last checked Software Update and see whether it was successful
- Set your Mac to check for updates weekly, daily or monthly from pull down menu
- Tick to download only the most important updates automatically
- (Installed Updates) See the Name and Date of installed updates with the appropriate version
- Open this "history" as a Log File (text rich document)

Speech

Speech is probably one of the most little understood features (preferences) on Everyman Jack's Mac. That is, if there were a fraternity of Mac users in the same room and you asked, "What is one preference you never use or don't understand on your Mac?" nine out of ten would say this Speech preference. Given the unanimity of this, here is our best attempt to explain (how to use) the Speech preference:

- (Speech Recognition) Turn speakable Items ON/Off
- Calibrate Microphone
- Change the Listening Key (Esc is default)
- Choose to Listen only when this key is pressed
- Tick the Speak command acknowledgement and change the sound from the scroll down menu (you can also choose "none")
- Change the Command set under the smaller "Commands" button
- (Text to Speech) Change the system voice and Play
- Change the speaking rate (How fast the text will be read)
- Tick or un-tick certain alerts and set them
- Open the Date & Time or Universal Access preference from this Pane to change the settings

Time Machine

Time Machine is a cool name for a cooler feature that comes pre-installed on every Leopard running Mac machine. For the first time in computer history, you can now go back in time to an early version of a file (a *Word* .doc file for example) and retrieve it. If you remembered how much better an article was last week than this week, you can go back to the exact day (time, minute, second) and read and retrieve it. Or, if you've accidentally deleted a picture from your wife's photo album, then you can retrieve it pre-rubbish bin. And, the coolest feature of Time Machine is that you don't have to think about (or remember) to back these files up. If you've got Time Machine ON (with proper hardware attached), your Mac will save all your "work" instinctually. The Time Machine preference allows you to do some neat intricate set-ups.

- Turn Time Machine ON/Off with the little light flip switch under the big icon to the left
- Tick to show the Time Machine icon in the Menu bar
- See the Name, Oldest Backup, Latest Backup and Next Backup time
- Change the Disk (exterior driver, for example) where Time Machine backs files up
- See what Time Machine does (in the grayed box below)
- Choose your Options as to when you'd like Time Machine to save your work

Universal Access

Universal Access is the easy way to set up a Mac for someone with a number of handicaps. Universal Access is, by name, giving those of different abilities the ability to access programs and do things on a computer. Universal access, developed in 2005 by Apple, helps the blind, deaf and handicapped. There are four components under the Universal Access preference: Seeing, Hearing, Keyboard and Mouse & Trackpad. Under each of these, there are multiple subcomponents that allow the user to change the Options of their Mac.

- (Seeing) Turn VoiceOver ON/Off
- Turn Zoom ON/Off
- Change the display colors and grayscale and contrasts with the slide rule
- Show Universal Access in Menu bar
- Enable access for assistive (external) devices
- (Hearing) Turn on the flash screen when an alert sounds

- Test the flash screen (gets the user's attention)
- Adjust the Volume
- (Keyboard) Turn Sticky Keys ON/Off
- Tick or un-tick preferences for key combinations
- Tick or un-tick Slow Keys and set to repeat key
- (Mouse & Trackpad) Turn mouse keys ON/Off
- Change the delay speed of the mouse pointer with the scroll bar
- Change the max speed of the delay
- Ignore the trackpad to use other devices (mouse)
- Change the cursor size with the scroll bar
- Enable and change the keyboard preference

Ch. 11 Chapter Eleven: From iGadgets To iGizmos

The Instruments of Apple

The Differences & What They Do

Apple has come up with some fantastic gadgets and gizmos over the years. Perhaps this alone has been the reason of their growing success. In fact, Apple pretty much owns the MP3|4 player market with the advent of the iPod in 2001 and the selling of the 100 millionth iPod in 2007. Just when you think Apple is lying dormant, they create the iPhone in 2007, with 2.3 million sold in 2008 (quarter 1) alone. And, the thing is, Apple plans on making these gadgets even better, from more user-friendly to (hopefully) more affordable.

This chapter on Apple's gadgets will let you know what you can do with your new iGizmo (and the applications involved), some simple tips and tricks and anything pertinent to software. We'll try, too, to tell you how the gadget works with Leopard OS and if you'll have any problems. Well further discuss international restrictions and/or usages where necessary.

Apple's iPhone

The iPhone is apple's newest portable gizmo, allowing users to talk on the phone, use it like a widescreen iPod and connect wirelessly (using 3G technology) to the Internet. More than a cell phone, the iPhone is a highly interactive, touchscreen smartphone, camera, media player, text messaging device, visual voicemail, E-mail, web-browsing and wi-fi supercenter. Plus, the virtual keyboard automatically corrects common misspellings. The iPhone is everything you need and want in our techno-centric life, gone portable.

Précis of (Vital) Programs

Phone:
The Phone Application on the iPhone allows you to make a call by tapping the name or number on the menu. If you want to quickly flip through your contact list, all you have to do is flick your finger. You can play your voicemails in any order or by selecting them from the appropriate list. And, the coolest feature of iPhone allows you to tap any number or name—say in your E-mail contacts or from an SMS message—and your iPhone will instantly dial the number for you. You can import/export your contacts to/from your Mac.

Calculator:
This feature on the iPhone gives you a full touchscreen calculator, both basic and scientific with a simple iPhone rotation. (Anytime you rotate the iPhone, the screen enables better viewing or more advanced options.)

Camera:
With Leopard, the photos you take with your iPhone syncs with iPhoto on your Mac and vice-versa. You simply take a picture with the tap of a button. Once they are taken, they'll appear in the picture library. Next time you connect to your computer, the photos are put in sync. One of the cool things is geotags that allow you to have info about the wheres and whens of the picture.

Mail
Unlike most phones, iPhone lets you access your Emails from all the most popular servers. Plus, it won't look all shoddy and stripped either. The iPhone lets you see Email as it would appear, say, on your desktop or laptop. Moreover, you can receive Emails from work really fast with automatic arrival. The iPhone is good for play but, most importantly, for business.

Maps
You've most likely used Google! Maps to either search out a location or used it to get directions from point A to B. Well, the iPhone now comes standard with GPS, suing cell tower locaters to tell you where you're at and where to go within a few feet. You can zoom in or out, scan or view as satellite, terrain or road settings (or a combo of each).

iPod
Yes, we all new Apple could do it—include iPod technology with the iPhone—and they pulled through. Just when you think Apple is out to

take all your money, they give you both in one cool machine. Now, you can take your favorite songs, TV episodes and movies with you. Added to this, you can watch those great shows in widescreen with a simple turn of the iPhone.

iPhone: Tips & Tricks

The iPhone has so many little tricks that you may think you know them all by now. However, we've provided some of the lesser (must we say "secret") prongs to help you lube your iPhone experience. And, these are OK to do in public. Here are the top six **iPhone** tips:

Tip **i**: If you think that getting to the top of that micro-web page is a drag—literally, dragging your finger or pointer to the top—then try this tip. All you have to do is tap the menu bar at the top of the screen (the one that shows the time and airport bars). You can do this in Safari too, which will take you to the top and bring up URL text field so you can type in a new web address.

Tip **P**: If you're unlike most Americans and write in more than one language, then you can access a variety of characters for, say French or Spanish. In order to do this, all you have to do is hold down the letter on the virtual keypad. If, for example, you need an E with an accent (that little line over the top, like in Café), then hold down the E key. With this, you'll get at least five different Es to choose from.

Tip **H**: If you see a link (a blue word with a line underneath it), and you'd like to see the web address without navigating to that page, then here's a simple trick. All you have to do is scroll over the link word and hold it. The URL will appear as a little balloon, giving you the web address and URL. This keeps you from going forward and backwards between web pages.

Tip **O**: If there's one feature Mac users really like on their Macs, it's got to be the screenshot capability. Well, surprise, you can do the same with your iPhone. If you'd like to take a screenshot picture, then hold the Home button and then click the Sleep button. You'll see a flash of white (like someone hits you over the head), and the screenshot will be taken. You can find it in the camera roll (default), unless you've changed this setting.

If there's an image (picture for example) that you like, you can save that too (without taking a screenshot). If you're in Safari, press and hold the image you'd like to save. Two options will then magically appear on the forefront of your screen. You can choose to Save Image or Cancel. If saved, you can save it in your camera roll. Later, you can keep that image forever, Email it or make it the backdrop of your iPhone screen.

Tip **N**: If you don't like the way your icons are arranged, then you can change these. If you'd like to move an icon from the gray bottom dock bar, then you can do so. Simply hold down the icon. When the icon starts shaking, you can move it anywhere on the Home screen. When complete, press the Home button and the icon will be moved. You can put up to four different icons in the dock at the bottom.

Tip **E**: Sometimes you'll be on a webpage—say a Dog Grooming Blog or the NY Times—and can't for the life of you read the text. There's an easy way to zoom on any text on any webpage. If you double tap the column about the Economic Failure, for example, then the words will fit in the width of the iPhone screen. Essentially, by tapping a picture, a certain word or column in a newspaper or blog, you're telling iPhone to fit-topage, making the "area" tapped more readable.

iPhone Software

The first software that came pre-loaded on your iPhone worked seamlessly with Apple created programs and applications. The problems, however, started when users who wanted more from their iPhone began downloading more and more third-party applications. Some of these proved to be a little much for the iPhone to handle all at once. Reports by the trunk full started describing lost signals, dropped calls and trouble getting Emails from POP accounts. Here's how to upload the newest version of iPhone's software so you won't have to deal with these side effects.

- Make sure you have the newest version of iTunes installed on your computer. At the time of writing, this is iTunes version 8. (Open iTunes and select Check for Updates…)
- You'll then want to connect your iPhone to your computer (or vice versa)
- From the Source List, select your iPhone
- You can click for updates once you check for them under the summary section
- All you'll have to do now is download the newest software and let it automatically install to your iPhone

This newest software can fix various problems you may have been encountering with your iPhone software. Checking and installing updates is highly recommended as you'll get better battery life, faster application installation, less crashes, better 3G (or more) signals, better text messaging and an overall smoother running system.

iPhone Usage

The iPhone is sold with a SIM card lock to AT&T. This means that users have to use AT&T in order to use the iPhone and all its features within the United States. Though AT&T says that the iPhone cannot be unlocked, even if you do not have a contract, almost 25% of iPhone users do not use AT&T as their provider. Essentially, these minorities have figured out a way to "unlock" the SIM card and use another wireless provider, such as Verizon.

International lawsuits—especially in Europe and Australia—began popping up against this SIM card lock. If the SIM card is unlocked, the media player and web features are not supposed to work if not authenticated and activated in a verified store. Of course, however, hackers have figured out a way to bypass these lock and safety features.

Apple suggests that such iPhone were perhaps shipped and unlocked abroad. Whatever the case, it is now possible to unlock the iPhone if you do not want to use AT&T, though the legality of such moves are still in question. In many countries, it is illegal to "lock" a SIM card to a provider, so the "unlock" must be legal.

In the US, it is said that a man by the name of Jon Lech Johansen published his custom software and iTunes binaries to help people unlock their iPhone. If you wish to bypass AT&T and use another network, make sure you know what you're doing and the implications involved. Perhaps ordering your iPhone from Europe or purchasing one abroad might not be an infringement of any sort. These are just some suggestions and not recommendations, though other options are available.

Apple's iPod

Apple gave the mobile-music-listener-device life when it introduced the iPod in 2001. With the advent of the iPod 2G, 3G and 4G in 2002, 2003, and 2004 respectively, Apple started literally branching off with other, cooler and more befitting iPods around 2004, with the iPod mini for example. Later in 2004 we got the U2 iPod and in 2005 we were graced with the iPod nano and iPod color.

A year later, the iPod shuffle got tiny music players into millions of hands (and ears). Apple introduced the iPod Touch or (unofficially called) iTouch in 2007. It allows users to simply touch the screen to run applications and play music/videos/podcasts without the big touch wheel taking up possible screen space.

iPod Third-Party Programs

The new iPod touch comes with a great deal of (what apple calls) "Fun." This is to say that you can do more on the iPod touch than any other erstwhile iPods. From WiFi gaming to watching movies in widescreen to creating smart playlist at a touch of the screen, the iPod has come a long way since 2001.

If, however, you are interested in doing even more with your iPod, then it is possible to download third party applications. In order to do so, you'll have to jailbreak your iPod (look it up if necessary) and install a program manager, something like installer.app for instance.

By using this, you'll be able to install, update and remove third-party programs on your iPod. You'll have tons of choices to truly customize your iPod the way you want. The online community for such hacking is growing, so you won't be alone if you run into trouble. (This gives you an idea of what is out there, and may not be recommended. This usually nulls and voids any sort of warranties you might have with Apple. It is recommended to always use the Apple Support pages to download the latest and greatest Apple software out there.)

iPod: Tips & Tricks

There are a lot of ways to get the most out of your iPod. One of the easiest things that can help is to conserve battery power. Here are some ways to do so.

Since the iPod is about 80-85% charged in one-hour of charging, you should be OK to use it after an hour. If you want it fully charged, it might take 2-4 hours longer. Make sure your iPod is off when being charged.

Try to charge your iPod when it is fully dead. Don't charge it when it has 40% battery life, for instance.

If you're going to step away and leave your iPod unattended, be sure to push *Pause*. The iPod will keep playing if you don't. Plus, if you have it on repeat, it will play continuously until dead as well. You can shut the iPod off by holding the *Play* button.

You can choose to shut off the backlighting by going into *Settings.* Then, go into *Backlight Timer* and choose *OFF.* This saves you tons of energy.

Just the same, turn the Equalizer off by going into *Settings.* Then, choose *Equalizer* and *OFF.*

Try to use Playlist rather than going back and forth between songs and artists. This will make you use the Previous and Next buttons less, keeping the iPod hard drive off.

Try to charge your iPod at room temperature. Don't store it in the car on hot days. Keep it out of the sun too.

Most importantly, keep the Hold switch switched on (orange showing) whenever possible. Otherwise, the screen (and hard drive) will keep turning on when flopping around in your pocket.

Apple's Apple TV

It use to be so easy to sit down after dinner, walk over to the TV, turn the 27-channel dial, find something that wasn't snowed-out, give the bent bunny-ear antennae a twist and watch good ole *Andy Griffith* or *Gilligan's Island.* With not so many choices and less than perfect picture quality, the halcyon TV life of yesteryear brings tears to our eyes. Today, however, we have hundreds of channels to surf but nothing to watch. We are bombarded with commercials and given no break from late-breaking news. That is until Apple came out with Apple TV.

Apple TV is, again, Apple thinking of the future, setting new standards in entertainment and technology. With the Apple TV, you don't have to worry about snow, you don't have to worry about commercials and you don't have to worry about over-bombardment or missing your favorite programs.

Essentially, Apple TV is a media hub—with 20, 40 Gig and up available—that you connect to your HD TV. You can leave your Apple commuter in the family room or office and buy and play movies, songs, podcasts, photos and more wirelessly to your TV. You can even take music from your iTunes list and play it on your TV's surround sound speakers. Your TV becomes more than a television TV, it becomes a supervision TV— never before so versatile yet so user-friendly.

Apple TV Program Software

When Apple TV first came out, the software was Apple's Front Row media. This software was originally used for the Mac, a simple way to load and play anything from Podcasts to movies. The newest Apple TVs, however, don't use this anymore. The people at Apple decided that the iPod look suited the Apple TV much better—perhaps trying to give iTunes, the iPod and the Apple TV (formerly iTV) a more ubiquitous look. With Apple TV now, you'll get all your iTunes library choices appearing under their respective menus. At any rate, here's a breakdown of what you can do with latest software running on your Apple TV.

Playing Movies

- Unlike iTunes, you can change the language, add subtitles or watch and listen to commentaries with Apple TV.

- You can sync movies (and all other media) from your Apple TV to your computer, to your iPod, to your iPhone and so on. You can add music from your Apple TV to your computer and then iPod wirelessly within minutes. Any combination of syncing with any of your Apple media libraries will work seamlessly.

- Rent or buy standard or HD movies. Put those on your computer or Apple TV or iPod and watch them within 30 days for up to 24 hours. Once you push play, for instance, you could watch a two-hour movie 12 times in one day.

- In the movie summary screen, you can choose from your favorite directors and actors and find other movies they have been in. You can then look them up by Top Movies, Genres and Newest Releases.

- You can even watch YouTube videos on your TV screen. You can bookmark your favorites and search the Top Rated to the Most Viewed, all from your Apple TV.

Playing TV Shows

- It's now possible to watch your favorite—new and old—TV shows without commercials. Because you pay money (a dollar or two usually), then you get to watch thousands of choices at the push of a button. Plus, they're yours forever.

- Many of the episodes you buy are HD, giving you the best quality money can buy.

- You can buy entire seasons, day passes and multi-passes that give you access to shows that air daily. You can even watch those at your convenience. Apple TV waves good-bye to Tivo and such technology.

- You can sync all your favorite shows to your iPhone, iPod and computer anytime.
- You can use Parental Controls—just like on your Mac—by setting up an administer password. This allows you to set certain restrictions on media content that may not be suitable for your youngling.

Playing Music

- Now you can watch and listen to your favorite music videos and music through your home's surround sound system. You can even control it wirelessly using your iPhone as a remote control by downloading the Remote application for iPhone at the Apple Support site.
- If you've got the newest version uploaded, you can have Genius create a playlist for you. Genius automatically takes the music you listen to most, create a playlist it thinks you'd enjoy and starts playing for you.
- You can upload your iTunes library to Apple TV or vice versa. You can add, delete and create new playlists on one and sync it later to another. The possibilities are flexible and endless.

Skimming Photos

- You can skim through your photos in bigger and better quality now. You can even keep albums on your Apple TV or take them from your computer.
- You can set up a screensaver-like display or simply view the thumbnails of pictures. You can set albums to music and watch them in random order.
- You can save photos on your Apple TV and remove them from your Mac if necessary too.
- And, of course, all the pictures in all your Apple iGizmos can be synced whenever you want.

Listening to Podcasts

- A Podcasts allows you to listen to informative talks, school lessons or media coverage all from your home computer using iTunes. Now, though, you can listen to your favorite ones from your Apple TV.

- Listening to Podcasts never was so easy. Now, some are available in HD. Others, however, are simply for your listening enjoyment. All, though, are free.

- You can even create your own Podcasts on your Mac, and make it available to your TV in a matter of minutes.

Apple TV Tips & Tricks & Warnings

- Stream live your media in your iTunes library to your Apple TV then to the TV for bigger and better viewing.

- You may not need Airport Extreme like the box says if your Internet connection is Wi-Fi 802.11-b, -g, or –n. An Ethernet connection of 10/10-BASE-T is also fast enough to stream media to your Apple TV.

- You'll get a small Apple Remote in the box. You don't necessarily need an iPhone with the Remote Application to wirelessly run your Apple TV.

- Though Apple says the USB port on the back of the Apple TV is for diagnostic purposes only, you can use it as an Ethernet port. If you've got a USB2 cable, you can connect your computer directly to the Apple TV box.

- You can change the resolution on your Apple TV to 1080i, 720p, 480p and 576p.

- The cables you'll need to connect to your TV are sold separately. Take note of this before you go home without them.

- If you have homemade videos, you can play them on Apple TV—AS long AS they play on your iPod, they should be OK to play on your Apple TV.

- If you've got an older TV, Apple TV may not be compatible. You may have to upgrade to a whole new TV before it will work. Change is good but can be costly.

- With some work, hacking and research, it is now possible to run Mac OS X on your Apple TV. This gives you more versatility. You'll have to do this yourself if you're interested, however.

- Apple says Apple TV will work in Europe.

Ch. 12 Chapter Twelve: From iGizmos to iWireless

The Wireless (less messy) Apple

The Wireless Options for Your Mac

Do early morning conversations with your partner start something like this: "Honey, have you seen my iPod charger?" "Sweetheart, did you put my iPhone USB cable somewhere?" "I'm late. Where's my Mac USB extension?" These questions go on and on, but the wires…oh, the wires, they don't have to go on and on. That's right, you can actually buy another iGizmo and never deal with (and possibly lose) any wires, cables or cords ever again (well, mostly).

Apple has really set The standard for gizmos—from music players to mobile internet phones to how information is collected, gathered, stored and used. The same holds true in Apple's attempt to get rid of the bird nests of wires and replace them with the cobweb networks of wireless connectivity. Here are some things in this chapter that may or may not come with your Mac to make your life iWireless.

Apple's Time Capsule

We've talked about Time Machine in various chapters of this manual, so you probably get the gist of this neat Mac Application by now. If not, Time Machine is a way to automatically backup your computer files onto an exterior hard drive. It can save everything for you from every hour to every week or whatever your preference. If ever you lose, misplace or delete a file, you can simply go back through Time Machine and retrieve it at any time (literally going back in time). You can therefore find the current copy verbatim or go back to the day (or time) you first created the file.

Apple's Time Capsule works with Time Machine in order to help you not only automatically back up your files but also carry no heed to file size (given that you're a home [common] computer user). The Time Capsule is not a file but a hardware unit you can place pretty much anywhere inside your home or office and use with Leopard OS X.

What Can Time Capsule Do For Me?

Time Capsule can help you take those files you've got so dearly secured in the hard drive of your Mac and hold them forever in storage.

And, the cool thing about this storage is that it's all done wirelessly. And, the even cooler thing is that more than one computer can use the Time Capsule base simultaneously to store and back up files from any home networked computer.

The Time Capsule can either hold 500 Gig of information or up to 1 TB. All your family's computers can be backed-up in one little white box. Moreover, Time Capsule can stand in for a Wi-Fi station for your home or home office, with plenty of ports for Ethernet WAN (DSL or Cable) or LAN devices.

What Can Time Capsule Do?

In addition to working with you, the Time Capsule can work for you. One of the leading features of Time Capsule is the ability to have a networked hard drive in your home or office. That is, you can store files on Time Capsule and someone else can have secondary access to them (as long as you let them). You can store and share files easily over networked computers so you don't have to waste time uploading and downloading from the Internet. Plus, everyone can print to one printer without having wires and cords strung everywhere. And, to boot, you can use Time Capsule with iPhone, Apple TV and iPod touch.

Apple's Airport Extreme

The Airport Extreme by Apple fixes a lot of home networking complications. Unlike Time Capsule, the Airport Extreme is a dummy-down and cheaper version for people not needing the extra wireless hard drive. What this does, however, is allow up to 50 users access to a network (get on the Internet, for example) at once.

What Can Airport Extreme Do For Me?

The good thing about Aiport Extreme is you won't need to run the latest and greatest version of Leopard OS X—say your school or kids' computers aren't upgraded yet— you'll all still be able to use the same network wirelessly; and, with the multiple data streams (going in and out through various antennas) you'll all be able to hotfoot it simultaneously through any number of web pages.

What Can Airport Extreme Do?

There are a few good tricks the Airport Extreme can perform. If students are in a classroom, for example, they'll be able to access the teachers Shared Hard Drive to have access to syllabi and worksheets. Once complete, the student can then print out the work wirelessly and hand it in to the teacher. Plus, the 802.11n (a fancy number for higher speed networking) gives all the students equal speeds on the network. And, even the kids in the back of the room will have access as the range is in many cases two to five times stronger.

Apple's Airport Express

The Airport Express is essentially a mini-me version of the Airport Extreme. You can use it as a household networking device or take it on the road to pick up that weak hotel Wi- Fi signal. By plugging in the Express into a 110-Volt outlet, a simple home (or office) network is created. If you are lucky enough to have a family of ten, for instance, you'll all be able to use the Airport Express at once. Additionally, you'll not only be able to print to one printer wirelessly, but you'll be able to play iTunes using Air Tunes anywhere in the house. The Airport Express is about the same size as a Mac laptop plug-in unit.

What Can Airport Express Do For Me?

Apple's Airport Express is good if you travel a lot or need a portable wireless amplifier. In other words, say for example, you stay in a lot of hotels. These hotels say they have Wi-Fi but the signal can be weak. By plugging in the Airport Express into an outlet, the signal will be made stronger so your Mac can pick it up easier. The signal becomes stronger and you can finally complete those online company profiles before the next day's meeting.

What Can Airport Express Do?

Airport Express can also play your computer's music anywhere in the house. By using iTunes and AirTunes, you'll be able to have the upstair's computer play over speakers downstairs. All you have to do is plug in a set of speakers into the Airport Express earphones jack and away you go. Pump up the jam in any part of your house wirelessly from any one of your home's computers.

Apple's Bluetooth

Apple uses Bluetooth technology in nearly all their igizmos these days. Heck, it's even in the newest iPods. Put simply, Bluetooth is for shorter distances but negates the needs for all those clumsy, trip-you-up wires. Essentially, all those little gadgets that keep you connected to the virtual world—from computers to iPhones to mobile phones and hands free ear phones—without having to plug one thing into another and vice versa. Through Bluetooth, devices can connect wirelessly in a range of thirty feet or less. You can even share songs and trade picture libraries using Bluetooth.

What Can Bluetooth Do For Me?

Bluetooth can make your life both hands and wires free. You've most likely walked through an airport or down Main Street and seen people with a Star-Trek-ish earpiece. This earpiece is actually connected via Bluetooth to their cell phone, probably strapped to their belts. The person can talk through this earpiece without using their hands. Plus, they don't have to worry about a swinging wire when they walk. This is just one of the many practical examples of what Bluetooth can do for you. Using a Mac, the Bluetooth technology only gets better.

What Can Bluetooth Do?

For starters, Bluetooth can connect your mobile phone to the Internet through your computer. Additionally, you can exchange files, say songs or a picture, to/from one mobile device to another using Bluetooth. It's possible too to sync your computer and hand-held palm device. You can connect to printers or faxes wirelessly and even use a keyboard or mouse wirelessly. Most new Macs—say in the last two years—come with Bluetooth technology. If not, you can buy portable USB Bluetooth modules and connect other enabled Bluetooth devices.

Apple's Wireless Keyboards and Mice

Though there are other brands of wireless keyboards and mice out there, Apple makes their own specifically for your Mac. That is, you can usually buy a wireless mouse at your local Wally-World; however, you'll have to plug in a "base" remote unit and USB connector. Yes, the keyboard and mouse are "wireless" but there is still a base, plug-in and USB device to attach to your computer. Apple's wireless keyboard and mouse, on the other hand, use the abovementioned Bluetooth wireless technology to eliminate the need for wires, plug-ins, cables or USB devices.

What Can Apple's Wireless Keyboard and Mouse Do For Me?

Using System Preferences and then Keyboard and Mouse Preferences, you'll be able to first pair your mouse and then pair your keyboard using just your computer. This means that you can have a truly wireless keyboard and mouse, signature-paired to your computer and its devices. If you've got battery power, then you've got work power, as you'll be able to sit back, relax and type and use your mouse almost anywhere in the room. Heck, hook up a Monster Cable to your Mac and you could use the TV as your monitor and finish that presentation all from your hotel bed.

What Can Apple's Wireless Keyboard and Mouse Do?

The wireless keyboard and mouse uses Bluetooth technology to pair with your computer. They keyboard and mouse both use AA batteries and do last for quite a long time (generally three months for the mouse and nine months for the keyboard). You can set up the keyboard, moreover, to perform certain functions more quickly. The keyboard, however, does not have any USB ports and does have some issues with startup key commands. On the same token, the Apple keyboard and mouse require Macintosh OS X 10.2.6 or later. They will neither work on Windows run computer nor in earlier version of Mac OS X.